NEW VANGUARD 258

ITALIAN CRUISERS OF WORLD WAR II

MARK STILLE   ILLUSTRATED BY PAUL WRIGHT

OSPREY PUBLISHING
Bloomsbury Publishing Plc

PO Box 883, Oxford, OX1 9PL, UK
1385 Broadway, 5th Floor, New York, NY 10018, USA
Email: info@ospreypublishing.com
www.ospreypublishing.com

OSPREY is a trademark of Osprey Publishing

First published in Great Britain in 2018

© Osprey Publishing 2018

A catalog record for this book is available from the British Library.

Print ISBN: 9781472825353
eBook ISBN: 9781472825360
ePDF ISBN: 9781472825346
XML ISBN: 9781472825377

18 19 20 21 22   10 9 8 7 6 5 4 3 2

Index by Fionbar Lyons
Typeset by PDQ Digital Media Solutions, Bungay, UK
Printed and bound by Bell & Bain Ltd., Glasgow G46 7UQ

The Woodland Trust
Osprey Publishing supports the Woodland Trust, the UK's leading
woodland conservation charity. Between 2014 and 2018 our donations
are being spent on their Centenary Woods project in the UK.

www.ospreypublishing.com
To find out more about our authors and books visit our website. Here you
will find extracts, author interviews, details of forthcoming events and
the option to sign up for our newsletter.

Acknowledgments
The author would like to extend his most sincere gratitude to Maurizio
Brescia who provided most of the photos for this book and provided
many points of clarification which made it immeasurably better.

Artist's note
Readers may care to note that the original paintings from which the
color plates in this book were prepared are available for private sale.
All reproduction copyright whatsoever is retained by the Publishers.
All inquiries should be addressed to: p.wright1@btinternet.com
   The Publishers regret that they can enter into no correspondence
upon this matter.

EXPLANATION OF THE NAMES OF ITALIAN CRUISERS

RM heavy cruisers were named after cities that had
been reunited with Italy following World War I.

Light cruisers were named after various warriors in
Italian history. Six of the 12 Condottieri light cruisers
were named after leaders of bands of mercenaries
which fought in the war between the Italian states from
the mid-14th until the 16th century. The second group
of Condottieri cruisers, consisting of *Luigi Cadorna* and
Armando Diaz, were named after the two leading Italian
generals of World War I. Later light cruiser names are:

Duca d'Aosta – named after the commander of the Third
Army in WWI.

Eugenio di Savoia – named after the famous Hapsburg
general who defended Vienna against the Turks in the
late 17th century.

Giuseppe Garibaldi – a 19th-century general and patriot
and a central figure in Italian independence.

Luigi di Savoia Duca degli Abruzzi – leader of expeditions
to Africa and the North Pole and WWI naval commander.

Ships of the Capitani Romani class were named after
notable generals and emperors of the Roman Empire.

CONTENTS

ITALIAN CRUISERS OF WORLD WAR II

INTRODUCTION

The Italian Royal Navy (*Regia Marina* or RM) operated one of the largest cruiser forces of World War II. Despite the myth that the RM shirked from battle during the campaign for control of the Mediterranean, Italian cruisers were active throughout the war and established several respectable combat records.

As a signatory of the 1922 Washington Naval Treaty, the RM immediately attempted to reinforce its treaty-limited battleship force with large 10,000-ton cruisers. Before the start of the war, the RM had built seven of these ships, eventually called heavy cruisers, giving them numerical parity with the French Navy. The first generation of RM heavy cruisers was not considered successful since they were deficient in protection, which would have impeded their ability to act as part of the battle line. However, the second generation of RM heavy cruisers was among the finest of the treaty period. Six of the RM's heavy cruisers were sunk during the war, including three in a single night against the British Royal Navy at the battle of Cape Matapan. Italian heavy cruisers were present at every major fleet engagement in the Mediterranean during the war.

Italian light cruisers possessed interesting design histories and were active throughout the war. Of the 12 completed before the war, six survived. These ships were in every major fleet engagement in the Mediterranean, as well as several smaller encounters with units of the Royal Navy. RM light cruiser designs initially favored speed over armor, but later classes possessed greatly improved protection. The final class of RM light cruisers, completed during the war, was really just large destroyers. Of the 12 ships planned, only three were completed before the armistice between Italy and the Allies in September 1943.

RM Naval Strategy and the Role of the Cruiser

The mission of the RM at the start of the war was to protect Italy from naval attack, keep sea lines of communications open to North Africa and Albania, close the Sicily Strait to Allied transit, and exercise sea control in the Central Mediterranean. It was not envisioned that the main fleet would fight in the Western or Eastern Mediterranean, leaving this to light forces. With few exceptions, the RM restricted main fleet operations to the Central Mediterranean. This led to the generally correct interpretation that the

RM was strategically timid but, as we shall see later, was aggressive on the operational level when British forces entered the Central Mediterranean.

Tactically, the RM desired to fight surface actions at long range. Accordingly, the Italians expected surface battles to start with a long-range gunnery phase. The RM's battleships, few in number, and its more numerous heavy cruisers, were the centerpiece of this phase. Gunnery in this phase would be conducted in a deliberate fashion, with a premium on observing the placement of salvos so fire could be adjusted. Only when salvos were observed to bracket the target would rapid fire be commenced. This tactic obviously depended on accurate fire at long range, which proved problematic for the RM during the war. RM doctrine called for a decisive short-range gunnery phase after the enemy had been weakened at long range. This was never realized during the war since long-range fire proved ineffective and because Italian commanders were often under orders not to risk their ships. Major fleet actions were expected to be fought during the day; there was no real training for night actions.

There were other reasons for the RM's tactical timidity. While the Italians traditionally planned a decisive battle for control of the Mediterranean, they also calculated that any large battle fought to a conclusion would be costly. The RM had little prospect of replacing heavy ships during the war, so there was an unspoken reluctance among naval commanders, and often direct orders from higher command, not to risk heavy ships. In almost every major battle involving cruisers, Italian on-scene commanders were handicapped by restrictive orders that they were not to engage a British force unless a clear superiority was evident. Given the difficulties of coordinating air reconnaissance with the Italian Air Force, and the almost universal unavailability of accurate and timely reconnaissance reports, the RM rarely fought sustained actions, even when it possessed superior strength.

Heavy cruisers were considered part of the fleet's battle line. RM light cruisers were used in a variety of ways. The most common use was to operate in divisions of two to four ships with the battle fleet. In fleet actions, they were used primarily in a scout role. Some light cruisers were also frequently used for transport missions. This became especially important during periods when British submarines and airpower began to take a heavy toll on convoys to North Africa. Fitted with the capability to carry large numbers of mines, RM light cruisers were also often used as minelayers.

RM CRUISER DESIGN

The Washington Naval Treaty of 1922 set the conditions which would affect all RM heavy cruiser construction. Italy was a signatory to the treaty, and while the number of cruisers that the Italians could build was not restricted,

This photograph shows *Zara* soon after commissioning. Note the aft 4.7-inch/47 twin mount still in place. (E. Bagnasco collection)

their size and armament was. The maximum size for a cruiser was set at 10,000 tons standard displacement, and its main battery could not be larger than 8-inch guns. The other European treaty signatories, France and the United Kingdom, began building treaty cruisers before the Italians, and since these foreign designs were at the treaty maximums, the RM felt it had no choice but to follow suit. The French Navy was seen as the RM's most likely future adversary, so the Italians were keen to surpass French designs. In addition, since the treaty put strict limits on battleship construction, and Italy did not have the required funds to embark on a new battleship program or even to modernize the battleships it already had, the construction of 10,000-ton cruisers, soon known as heavy cruisers, was seen as a substitute.

All treaty signatories had severe problems designing a balanced heavy cruiser which adhered to the 10,000-ton limit. Designers had to balance competing design priorities for firepower, protection, and high speed. The RM had traditionally valued high speed, and in order to perform one of its primary missions of scouting for the main battle fleet, Italian cruisers had to have a high maximum speed – well over 30 knots was desired. Firepower was also essential; the RM believed that if it had ships with superior speed and heavy firepower then it could engage an enemy force at long range and disengage at will. As a result, protection was not the initial design emphasis on Italian heavy cruisers, or later on light cruisers when they began to be built.

The first heavy cruisers, the Trento class, followed this mold. The top speed of the class was 35 knots and it carried a main battery of eight 8-inch guns. Protection, primarily measured in the form of armor on the main deck and the main belt, was on the light side, but was better than that of the first French heavy cruisers, which were virtually unprotected. RM designers achieved a greater level of protection on the Trento class by producing a ship 500 tons over the treaty limit. The second generation of Italian heavy cruisers, the four ships of the Zara class, addressed the lack of protection by sacrificing speed. The amount of armor went from 888 tons on the Trento class to 1,500 tons on the new class. However, the secret of this apparent design success was an even greater cheating of treaty limits by between 1,300 and over 2,100 tons (each of the ships in the class had a different displacement).

The two-ship Duca d'Aosta class built on the success of the Montecuccoli class by further increasing the level of protection. This is *Duca d'Aosta* at La Spezia in the late 1930s. (M. Brescia collection)

Luigi di Savoia Duca degli Abruzzi pictured in 1938. The ships of the Garibaldi class added more protection compared to the previous Duca d'Aosta class and also enjoyed a slightly larger main battery. There were also several major alterations in the configuration of the new class, including the closely spaced stacks, a pole mainmast instead of the earlier tripod masts, and a longer forecastle and quarterdeck. (E. Bagnasco collection)

Initial RM light cruisers were also driven by an imperative to better French designs. Like the RM's heavy cruisers, they initially stressed speed over protection. Incremental changes were made over the course of five different classes, which allowed the RM to eventually arrive at a balanced light cruiser design. The London Naval Treaty of 1930 introduced overall tonnage limits for heavy and light cruisers. It also distinguished between the two types of cruisers – heavy cruisers of up to 10,000 tons with a maximum of 8-inch guns and light cruisers of no set tonnage (however, the maximum limit of 10,000 tons still applied) with a maximum of 6.1-inch guns. The Italian government did not ratify the London Treaty, but still adhered to the most important parts of the treaty since it did not wish to destabilize the naval limitations system. The Italians did not build any additional heavy cruisers, so construction focused on light cruisers. The first two of the "Condottieri" class of cruisers were lightly protected and lightly constructed and proved generally unsatisfactory in wartime conditions. The next classes incrementally emphasized protection and produced much better balanced designs which performed well during the war. The final class of RM light cruisers, the Capitani Romani class, was an anomaly which was actually better described as large destroyers since they possessed no protection and carried a destroyer-type main battery. Despite this, and the fact that their standard displacement was only 3,686 tons, they were classified by the RM as light cruisers.

RM CRUISER WEAPONS AND FIRE CONTROL SYSTEMS

Overall, RM cruiser guns were reliable and the design of fire control equipment was excellent. However, there were several major problems which reduced the effectiveness of Italian naval gunnery. This meant the shells from a salvo were scattered over a wide area. Generally, the tighter the salvo, the greater the prospects of scoring a hit once the target had been bracketed. Excessive dispersion made accurate gunnery all but impossible. Many times during the war, British observers stated that Italian gunnery was accurate for range, but

Attilio Regolo, the first of the Capitani Romani class to commission, photographed in late 1942. The dazzle scheme does a good job of breaking up the ship's profile, but it is still clear that these ships more closely resembled large destroyers than light cruisers. *Regolo* played little part in the war, but did prove robust enough to survive a British torpedo attack on November 8, 1942. (A. Fraccaroli collection)

This 1936 photograph shows *Trento*'s "C" and "D" turrets trained to starboard. The 8-inch guns on the RM's heavy cruisers were placed on a single cradle to save weight which adversely affected their effectiveness. (N. Siracusano collection)

RIGHT
The forward 6-inch/53 gun turrets photographed on light cruiser *Da Barbiano*. As is clearly evident, the 6-inch guns shared the same cradle; mounting the guns so close together meant that their shells interfered with each other in flight and caused dispersion problems. (M. Brescia collection)

FAR RIGHT
This view aboard light cruiser *Montecuccoli* shows some of the standard weaponry aboard RM cruisers. In the middle of the picture is a twin 4.7-inch/47 mount. This was a dual-purpose weapon capable of engaging surface and air targets and comprised the secondary battery of all but one class of RM cruisers. In the foreground is a twin 37mm/54 light antiaircraft gun mount. (M. Cicogna collection)

with the salvos suffering from excessive dispersion, actual hits were quite rare.

The salvo dispersion problem was caused by the twin guns in a turret being mounted on a single cradle. With the guns mounted close together, the shells interfered with each other in flight. Added to this was the excessive muzzle velocity the RM favored to get longer ranges, and inconsistent powder charge performance. Adding to the RM's woeful wartime gunnery performance was the fact that prewar training was unrealistic and exercises infrequent. Night gunnery was not practiced, which became a major issue since the British sought night actions.

The 8-inch guns on RM heavy cruisers were mounted on a single gun cradle, meaning the guns were very close together in a twin turret. Light cruisers carried the 6-inch/53 gun developed by Ansaldo. These were also fitted into two-gun turrets and provided with a single cradle to save weight. Thus, they experienced the same salvo dispersal issues as the 8-inch guns. The dispersion problem was heightened by a very high muzzle velocity. The RM eventually reduced the muzzle velocity of this weapon to 2,789 feet per second, which reduced maximum range to 24,700 yards. The later 6-inch/55 gun was an improvement with its lower muzzle velocity and because each gun was mounted in an individual cradle. These were the same guns fitted as secondary batteries on the Littorio-class battleships. The 5.3-inch guns fitted aboard the late-war Capitani Romani class were not dual-purpose guns, which greatly limited the antiaircraft capabilities of these ships.

Antiaircraft capabilities were generally deficient, but this was masked by the fact that the RM's principal surface combatants rarely faced a heavy air threat. The standard cruiser medium-caliber antiaircraft weapon was the Model 1928 100mm/47 gun, which had a rate of fire of 8–10 rounds per minute and could elevate to 80–85 degrees for antiaircraft work. The gun was satisfactory, but its fire control system, originally acquired from the British, was dated. Italian doctrine was to use this weapon in a barrage fire mode since the gun was not suited for aimed fire. An indication of how effective the RM judged this system to be was the fact that before the war many ships had two of their twin 100mm mounts replaced by twin water-cooled 37mm/54 Breda guns. This weapon was developed in 1930 and became the standard light antiaircraft gun. The weapon was reliable, but was fed by a six-round magazine which reduced the rate of fire. The 37mm weapon was complemented by the prewar 13.2mm machine gun, which was later replaced by the 20mm/65 gun, which was fitted in twin and single versions. The 20mm/70 Model 1939 was also used and was fitted aboard cruisers in a single pedestal-mounted version.

RM Cruiser Weapons

Type	Shell Weight (pounds)	Muzzle Velocity (ft/sec)	Max Range (yards)	Rate of Fire (rounds per minute)
8-inch/50 Ansaldo 1924 Model	276	2,969	34,256	3
8-inch/53 Ansaldo 1927/1929 Model	276	3,150	33,407	3–4
6-inch/53 Ansaldo 1926 Model	110	3,281	31,060	5
6-inch/55 Ansaldo 1934 Model	110	2,986	28,150	5–6
5.3-inch/45 OTO 1937 gun	72	2,707	21,430	6–7
100mm/47 OTO 1928 Model	30	2,789	16,670	8–10
37mm/54 Breda 1932	1.8	2,625	8,530	Maximum 200; actual 140
20mm/65 Breda 1935	.3	2,756	6,000	240

Fire Control Systems

The fire control table (computer) equipment aboard RM cruisers was based on the British Barr and Stroud system. The system was later produced in Italy under license, and there was a separate version for heavy and light cruisers. The system was relatively simple and fed target course and speed to the director.

Typically, RM cruisers carried two fire control directors. The primary one was mounted high on the forward superstructure or mast, and the second, which was used as a back-up, was placed lower on the superstructure. Each fire control director was equipped with a rangefinder. On heavy and light cruisers, the rangefinder was a Galileo coincidence set, 16.4 feet in length, which was designed to be effective out to 37,183 yards. Each director also had a stereoscopic scartometer to measure the distance that a shell fell from the target. On early heavy cruisers this was 9.8 feet in length; on light cruisers 16.4 feet.

The Montecuccoli class and later light cruisers were fitted with fixed directors above the bridge structure. These were equipped with two 23.6-foot rangefinders (now of a new type that combined coincidence and stereo). One of the rangefinders was used as a scartometer. The entire system was stabilized. On heavy cruisers, two smaller rangefinders (9.8 feet in length) were carried for the secondary battery.

RM CRUISER RADAR

The Italian electronics industry was unable to develop and produce modern radar equipment during the war. This placed the RM at a severe disadvantage, especially in night combat, since the British had equipped cruisers and battleships early in the war with radar. No RM cruisers were equipped with radar at the start of the war, and only a few ships received it in mid-1943 before the armistice. The first Italian-produced radar deployed operationally was the EC.3 "Gufo" (Owl). Only 12 of these were fitted before Italy's surrender in September 1943. This radar was used for both surface and air search, but was not accurate enough to permit radar-controlled gunnery. The EC.3 ter was the production version, but it was primitive compared to Allied equipment. The theoretical maximum range, subject to many operational and atmospheric conditions, was approximately 16nm against a large surface target and up to 50 miles against aerial targets.

Light cruiser *Eugenio di Savoia* received an EC.3 ter radar in 1943. At least two of the Capitani Romani light cruisers, *Scipione Africano* and *Attilio Regolo*, also received this radar. The shortage of Italian radars forced the RM to ask the Germans for assistance. Light cruiser *Abruzzi* received the German Fu.Mo 21/39 "De Te" in August 1943 and it was planned to fit the same radar on light cruiser *Aosta*, but this was stopped by the armistice in September 1943. The absence of radar was one of the RM's most critical operational deficiencies during the war.

RM CRUISERS AT WAR

The RM began the war with seven heavy cruisers and 12 modern light cruisers. These were assigned to the RM's two main squadrons; the First Squadron was usually centered around the battleships in service and the Second Squadron, with its flagship heavy cruiser *Pola*, centered around the heavy cruisers. Battleships and cruisers were organized into divisions; cruiser divisions consisted of usually three, but sometimes two, ships.

Italy entered the war on June 10, 1940, but the first major encounter between the RM and the British Mediterranean Fleet did not occur until the following month. As was usually the case during the naval war in the Mediterranean, any major clash was precipitated by one side reacting to the convoy movements of the other. In early July, the RM ran a major convoy to Benghazi in Libya, escorted by light cruisers *Bande Nere* and *Colleoni*. Meanwhile, the British were moving two convoys to Malta with the expectation of drawing the RM into a major engagement. The Italians were happy to oblige and send out the Second Squadron from ports in Sicily with six heavy cruisers, four light cruisers and 16 destroyers. This was

A All four Zara-class heavy cruisers took part in the first major naval battle of the Mediterranean War – the battle of Calabria (called the battle of Punta Stilo by the Italians) in July 1940. This scene shows two of these ships during the main gunnery phase of the action. This is the role for which the Zara class was designed; the RM planned that these heavily armored ships could take their place in the battle line and use their main battery to engage enemy ships at long range. In this view, they are firing their 8-inch guns at maximum elevation at unseen targets up to 28,000 yards away. At this range, the Italian cruisers scored no hits and the action ended indecisively.

supported by the First Squadron with two battleships, six light cruisers and 20 destroyers. Opposing the Italian battle fleet was a British force of three battleships, one aircraft carrier, five light cruisers, and 16 destroyers.

The Battle of Calabria (called the Battle of Punta Stilo by the RM)

The largest naval engagement of the Mediterranean War occurred on July 9, 1940. In the early afternoon, nine British torpedo bombers from the carrier *Eagle* unsuccessfully attacked three RM heavy cruisers. Light cruiser *Da Barbiano* spotted the British fleet at 1505 hours, and the action commenced at 1520 hours when the Italians opened fire at 23,600 yards. According to British accounts, Italian gunnery was generally accurate, but no hits were scored. At 1555 hours, heavy cruiser *Trento* engaged the British battleship *Warspite* at 28,000 yards. The British battleship was forced to change course after being bracketed. Meanwhile, *Warspite* hit the Italian battleship *Cesare* at 26,000 yards, and the Italian commander ordered his battle line to turn away and eventually break off the action. The Italian cruisers continued to engage *Warspite* with no effect while other RM cruisers dueled with their British counterparts. At 1605 hours, a British light cruiser hit *Bolzano* with three 6-inch shells, but she remained in action. Since most of the engagement was conducted at long range, it ended indecisively.

The Battle of Cape Spada

The next action involving RM cruisers demonstrated their salient weakness – lack of an ability to absorb damage. On July 17, light cruisers *Bande Nere* and *Colleoni* were dispatched to execute a hit-and-run raid against British tankers supposedly operating in the Aegean. This was the exact type of operation for which these fast and well-armed ships were designed. Instead of tankers, the cruisers spotted four British destroyers. The cruisers opened fire at long range against the fleeing British. The chase allowed a second British force with the Australian light cruiser *Sydney* and another destroyer to intervene. The Australian cruiser quickly scored a minor hit on *Bande Nere* and later hit *Colleoni* with three well-placed 6-inch shells. These jammed her rudder and destroyed the main steam line. The cruiser

B The RM's first cruiser loss occurred on July 19, 1940. At the battle of Cape Spada, light cruisers *Bande Nere* and *Colleoni* engaged a British force of one light cruiser (the Australian *Sydney*) and five destroyers. Unfortunately for the RM, this action demonstrated the inability of its early light cruisers to absorb significant damage as well as their inability to effectively employ their 6-inch guns. The Italian force was dispatched to execute a surprise raid against British tankers supposedly in the Aegean Sea, but instead the Italian commander allowed himself to be surprised by four British destroyers early on the morning of July 19. The cruisers gave chase and opened fire at long range at the fleeing British. From 0627 hours at an opening range of 19,000 yards, until 0648 hours, the Italians maintained a steady fire but hit nothing. At 0730 hours, *Sydney* intervened, and by 0746 hours the Italian commander turned to the southwest and made smoke to disengage with the two sides exchanging long-range gunfire. At 0821 hours, one of the Italian cruisers placed a 6-inch shell on *Sydney*, but it only blew a hole in the cruiser's forward stack, wounding one man. In exchange, *Sydney* hit *Colleoni* with three 6-inch shells at 0825 hours. These crippled the cruiser, since one shell destroyed the main steam line which brought the ship to a stop. Destroyer *Ilex* closed the wounded cruiser and hit her with a torpedo which blew off the cruiser's bow. *Colleoni* capsized at 0859 hours, but the British ships saved 545 of her crew. *Bande Nere* escaped after two 6-inch shell hits from *Sydney* failed to slow her down. During the action, the Italians fired 500 6-inch shells and scored only the single ineffectual hit on *Sydney*. This scene shows *Colleoni* firing at the unseen *Sydney* just before the Italian cruiser received her fatal damage.

Gorizia pictured in heavy seas in the Ionian Sea on the afternoon of September 1, 1940. This was one of many occasions that the RM's battle fleet put to sea but was forced to return without making contact with British forces. The water over the bow of the cruiser demonstrated the vulnerability of the Ro.43 floatplane on the bow catapult. (E. Leproni collection)

slowed to a halt and was soon hit by a destroyer-launched torpedo which blew off her bow. Another torpedo hit was later scored; the cruiser sank with the loss of 121 crewmen. *Bande Nere* escaped, being hit by another 6-inch shell from *Sydney*. Over the course of the action, lasting three hours, the Italians fired 500 6-inch shells and scored a single hit on *Sydney*. In return, the RM lost its first cruiser of the war.

On August 31, the RM's entire battle fleet – four battleships, 13 cruisers, and 39 destroyers – sortied to engage a Royal Navy convoy headed for Malta. No contact was made and, following his orders, the Italian commander returned to port that evening. Other sorties by the RM's battle fleet on September 7–9 and September 29–October 1 also made no contact.

The entire RM battle fleet was caught in Taranto on the night of November 11–12 by a British carrier air raid. Though only 21 aircraft were used in the raid, the results were spectacular. Three battleships were torpedoed and placed out of action. One never returned to service. Heavy cruiser *Trento* was hit by a bomb which did not explode. It is a myth that the disaster at Taranto removed the RM's willingness to fight; on November 17, when a Royal Navy carrier force departed Gibraltar to fly 12 aircraft to Malta, the Italians sent a force of two battleships, six cruisers and 14 destroyers to intercept. The British chose to avoid an engagement and they launched the 12 aircraft 400 miles from Malta but only four arrived safely (the other aircraft succumbed to fuel exhaustion).

The Battle of Cape Spartivento (called the Battle of Capo Teulada by the RM)

Just days later, the Italians again sortied their battle fleet to intercept British convoys headed for Malta. The combined RM force consisted of two battleships, heavy cruisers *Pola*, *Fiume*, *Gorizia*, *Trieste*, *Trento*, and *Bolzano*, supported by 14 destroyers. The Italian commander was again severely hamstrung by orders to only engage under the most favorable circumstances, and by conflicting and time-late reporting from air reconnaissance. The Italians decided to engage the British force coming from Gibraltar, which included one battleship, one battlecruiser, five cruisers (one heavy), and ten destroyers. The resulting battle of Cape Spartivento began on November 27 when *Pola*, *Fiume*, and *Gorizia* engaged British cruisers at 24,000 yards, joined minutes later by the other three heavy cruisers. On this occasion, the Italians shot accurately, with *Pola* scoring a hit on one of heavy cruiser *Berwick*'s 8-inch turrets, placing it out of action and starting a fire. A second shell hit *Berwick* aft. This hour-long long-range gunnery duel from between 16,000 and 23,000 yards was indecisive. The six RM cruisers fired between 27 and 210 rounds each, scoring only the two hits on *Berwick*. The British cruisers, supported by battlecruiser *Renown*'s 15-inch guns, scored no hits. The RM had performed well, but missed an opportunity to inflict a defeat on an inferior British force.

Disaster at Matapan

In 1941, the Germans entered the war in the Mediterranean. The immediate impact of this was that German air power closed off the Central Mediterranean to large British forces and that the RM was fully engaged in escorting convoys with German troops and supplies to North Africa. In early February, the British shelled the port of Genoa in northwest Italy, with a battleship, a battlecruiser, and a light cruiser, but the Italian fleet of two battleships, three heavy cruisers, and ten destroyers was unable to intercept.

Another result of German intervention was increased pressure for the RM to use its battle fleet more aggressively. After the Germans promised air support, the Italians decided to mount their first (and last) major operation into the Eastern Mediterranean. Assigned to the operation was a single battleship, six heavy cruisers, two light cruisers (*Abruzzi* and *Garibaldi*), and 17 destroyers. The plan called for three of the heavy cruisers and the two light cruisers to sweep into the Aegean Sea and the rest of the force to sweep off the southwestern coast of Crete. The Italians departed on March 26 under conditions of great secrecy. The battle of Matapan was underway.

By noon the next day, it was apparent to the Italians that they had lost the element of surprise, but the operation was not canceled. In fact, the British were well aware of the operation and had sortied a large force centered around three battleships and an aircraft carrier to intercept. On March 28, Italian aircraft spotted a British cruiser force near the Greek island of Gaudo (south of Crete), which turned to the west to fall back on the three British battleships. *Trieste*, *Trento*, and *Bolzano* gave chase and began a slow fire from extreme range. In 42 minutes, before turning away after failing to close on the British force, *Trieste* fired 132 8-inch rounds, *Trento* 214, and *Bolzano* 189. No hits were scored.

The Italian battleship succeeded in engaging the British cruisers, but with no effect. After enduring a British carrier air attack and suffering no damage, the Italian commander decided to return home. The three battleships of the British Mediterranean Fleet were well to the east of the Italian force, with no hope of engaging the Italians unless they were slowed by air attack. Throughout the afternoon and until last light, the British attacked the battleship and the six heavy cruisers with high-level bombers and torpedo aircraft. One torpedo hit was scored against the battleship, but she was able to resume a speed of 19 knots and looked sure to escape. In the last torpedo attack of the evening, one torpedo hit *Pola*, which knocked out all power and brought her to a stop.

Since the Italian commander had no idea that British units were close to the crippled *Pola*, he dispatched *Zara* and *Fiume* to assist and tow *Pola* if possible. As night fell, the situation became very confused, with both fleets divided into several groups. The critical moment came at 2210 hours, when radar aboard British battleship *Valiant* gained contact on *Pola*. Soon, *Zara*, *Fiume*, and four destroyers were detected in column coming to the aid of *Pola*. The British reacted more quickly, and brought the

The three Zara-class heavy cruisers lost at the battle of Matapan. From left to right is *Zara*, *Pola*, and *Fiume*. The ship in the rear is light cruiser *Duca degli Abruzzi*, which can be easily distinguished by her triple 6-inch gun turrets since she was the only RM cruiser to have a triple gun mount. The photograph was taken from light cruiser *Garibaldi* on the morning of March 27, 1941, the day before the disaster in which all the heavy cruisers in this photo were sunk. (E. Bagnasco collection)

C

POLA

Heavy cruiser *Pola* as she appeared at the time of her loss at the battle of Matapan in March 1941. *Pola* was designed as a flagship and had a larger bridge structure which was faired into the forward stack. In March 1941, the ship retained the prewar light gray overall scheme, with the addition of air recognition stripes on the forecastle. The track for the catapult fitted on the forecastle was a feature of all but one of the RM's heavy cruisers.

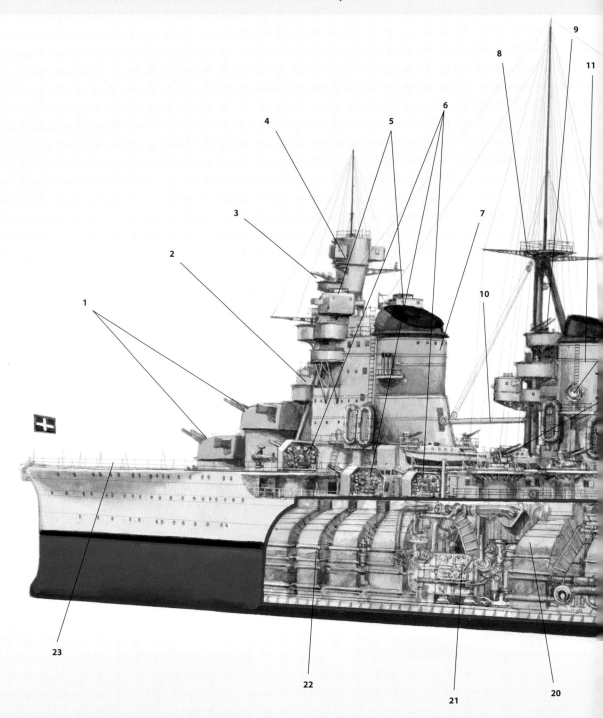

12

13   14

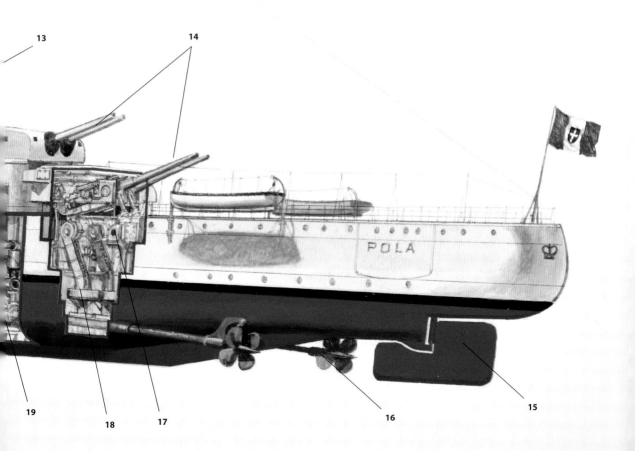

19   18   17   16   15

two cruisers under fire with 15-inch guns from the point-blank range of 3,000–4,000 yards. From this range, *Zara* and *Fiume* were quickly hit and devastated before they could return fire. Two of the destroyers were also hit and later sank. *Fiume* sank as a result of 15-inch shell damage, with the loss of 812 men. The drifting *Zara* was later finished off by destroyer-launched torpedoes and sank with 783 men. British destroyers found *Pola* dead in the water, and after taking off part of the crew, sank her with torpedoes. Another 328 men were lost. The battle was a total disaster for the RM and affected the conduct of the rest of the naval war in the Mediterranean.

During April and May, the RM concentrated on getting convoys through to Libya and laying defensive minefields. Since the supply of fuel oil was becoming critical, the RM's cruisers were only used sparingly to provide cover to the convoys. From January to June 1941, 94 percent of Axis cargos arrived safely. This dropped to 73 percent for the second half of the year. By September 1941, lack of oil was having a dramatic effect on RM operations. It was also at this time that the RM had five battleships in operation, giving it a clear advantage over the Mediterranean Fleet. The Italians decided to use this advantage and attempt a fleet action with the British forces operating from Gibraltar. This opportunity came in July when the British mounted a convoy to Malta from Gibraltar. Poor reconnaissance meant the Italian battle fleet never sailed. In August, two battleships, four heavy cruisers, and 19 destroyers did sail to intercept British forces coming from Gibraltar, but lingered south of Sardinia, and no contact was made with the British fleet. On returning to base on August 26, heavy cruiser *Bolzano* was torpedoed and seriously damaged by a British submarine.

In September, the Italians tried again to bring the Gibraltar-based forces into action. They sortied two battleships, three heavy cruisers, light cruisers *Abruzzi* and *Attendolo*, and 14 destroyers to intercept a large convoy headed to Malta. On September 27, the fleets got to within 40 miles of each other. With the British force of only two battleships, two light cruisers, and six destroyers, the RM would have had the advantage. Again, no engagement resulted when the Italian commander, thinking he was facing a superior force, broke off the operation.

In October, the British transferred two cruisers and two destroyers to Malta to intensify the threat to Italian convoys to Libya. In response, the RM had to assign cruisers to screen convoys. On November 9, the British force from Malta attacked a large convoy (known as the "Duisburg" convoy, from the name of a German ship in the formation) of seven merchant ships escorted by six destroyers. The British avoided action with the covering force of heavy cruisers *Trieste* and *Trento* and four destroyers and proceeded to shoot up the entire convoy, also sinking one of the escorts and damaging two more. The British exchanged fire with the two Italian cruisers after destroying the convoy; the Italians expended 207 8-inch shells and hit nothing. This was among the worst episodes of the war for the RM. It demonstrated its total failure to prepare for night action, highlighted the importance of radar (of which the RM still had none), and exemplified the impact of poor leadership. The British surface force operating from Malta savaged two more convoys, but encountered no RM cruisers in the process.

The difficulty getting supplies to Libya meant the RM was forced to use its older cruisers in a transport role. Accordingly, *Di Giussano* and *Da Barbiano* were each crammed with 950 tons of aviation fuel and 900 tons of other supplies and departed from Sicily to Tripoli, with orders to avoid any engagement. On December 13, the cruisers, together with one torpedo boat, were intercepted by four British destroyers. The night action opened with a destroyer putting two torpedoes into *Da Barbiano*. The cruiser was quickly hit by a third torpedo (and possibly another) and sank. *Di Giussano* was able to get three salvos off, but hit nothing. Within minutes, she was hit by a single torpedo and two 4.7-inch shells, which caused a large explosion and fire. The encounter, known as the battle of Cape Bon, was another disaster which again showed the marginal night-fighting capabilities of the RM.

First and Second Battles of Sirte

In late 1941 and for the first half of 1942, the Axis powers experienced a resurgence and dominated the Central Mediterranean. The RM was forced to make greater use of its remaining battleships and cruisers to provide cover for convoys to Libya. The first – Operation *M42* – included three battleships, heavy cruisers *Gorizia* and *Trento*, and ten destroyers as distant cover, with another battleship, three light cruisers, and three destroyers as close cover. This developed into an action with a British force of four light cruisers and 12 destroyers on December 17, which attempted to attack the Italian convoy. In this day action, the Italian heavy cruisers took the British under fire and inflicted slight damage on a destroyer. The Italians successfully protected their convoy, and two days later a British force of three cruisers and four destroyers ran into a minefield off Tripoli trying to re-attack the convoy. The minefield, laid by RM light cruisers, sank one cruiser and a destroyer, and damaged another cruiser.

The RM successfully ran several important convoys into Tripoli through March 1942, while keeping the pressure on Malta. In March, the British mounted another major operation to get a convoy through to Malta. On March 22, the RM dispatched a force of one battleship, heavy cruisers *Gorizia* and *Trento*, light cruiser *Bande Nere*, and seven destroyers to intercept the convoy as it tracked to the west from Alexandria. In a day action fought in extremely rough seas, the RM fought its best action of the war. The Italian commander hoped to trap the convoy between his battleship and a second group with the three cruisers. The action began at 1435 hours, with the cruisers opening fire from a range of 23,000 yards. No hits were scored, but that was not surprising given the sea conditions. The Italian battleship entered the action, which forced the British convoy to change course to the south instead of proceeding to Malta. *Bande Nere* scored a hit on British

Bande Nere was part of the RM force sent to engage the British convoy headed for Malta from Alexandria in March 1942. This photograph of the cruiser is from March 22, 1942 on the day the RM engaged the convoy's escort in the Second Battle of Sirte. (E. Bagnasco collection)

cruiser *Cleopatra*'s bridge at 1643 hours. Later in the action, *Gorizia* hit a British destroyer in her boiler room. Throughout the entire battle, the British scored a single 4.7-inch hit on the Italian battleship, while six British ships were damaged. More importantly, the convoy's arrival in Malta was delayed until the next day, allowing German aircraft to sink one of the four merchant ships short of the harbor; the other three were sunk after arriving in the harbor and only a fraction of their cargo was saved. In this battle, the RM had bested the British, with its cruisers playing an important role.

In April and May 1942, Italian convoys proceeded to Libya largely unimpeded. Pressure on Malta grew even more intense, which forced the British to mount another major convoy to the beleaguered island in June. On June 14, the RM's battle fleet of two battleships, heavy cruisers *Gorizia* and *Trento*, light cruisers *Garibaldi* and *Duca d'Aosta*, and 12 destroyers departed Taranto with plans to intercept the convoy the following morning. After maneuvering the convoy in hopes that aircraft and submarines would force the superior Italian force back to port, the British abandoned the operation on June 15. During this operation, *Trento* was damaged by an aircraft torpedo and then sunk by a British submarine while attempting to return to port.

The Battle of Pantelleria

Meanwhile, another British convoy was approaching Malta from the west. With its main effort directed against the eastern convoy, the RM had only light cruisers *Eugenio di Savoia* and *Montecuccoli* and five destroyers with enough fuel to contest the passage of the convoy coming from Gibraltar. On the morning of June 15, in the battle of Pantelleria, the Italians encountered the convoy escort of one light cruiser, five destroyers, and four destroyer escorts. The Italian force was outnumbered but did have the advantage of the superior range and firepower of the 6-inch guns on the two cruisers. These two cruisers gave a very good account of themselves in what was the best RM cruiser action of the war.

The action began with the two Italian cruisers opening fire on the five British destroyers at approximately 15,000 yards. On this occasion, Italian gunnery was deadly accurate – 12 6-inch shells hit destroyer *Bedouin*. Another 6-inch shell hit destroyer *Partridge*, damaging her machinery which brought her to a stop. Cruiser *Cairo* was also hit forward but suffered little damage. The three remaining British destroyers continued a gunnery duel with the Italian cruisers, and both sides suffered damage. Both RM cruisers took a hit and suffered minor damage.

Raimondo Montecuccoli at Genoa in early 1943 under repair from damage suffered on December 4, 1942 in Naples at the hands of USAAF heavy bombers. One bomb hit the ship near the forward stack and caused heavy damage that necessitated repairs lasting until July 31, 1943. (A. Fraccaroli collection)

After a period of maneuvering during which the Italian commander placed his force to the east of the convoy to block its passage to Malta, the gunnery duel resumed between the two RM cruisers and two of the British destroyers. The magazines of the Italian cruisers were running low on 6-inch shells after some 90 minutes of sustained firing. Meanwhile, at 0740 hours, another 6-inch shell hit *Cairo*, but did not explode. In the confusion and smoke, the Italians lost the convoy, but at 1123 hours the Italians sighted smoke to the southwest. These were two of the convoy's five merchant ships which had been damaged by air attacks and were in the process of being scuttled by the escorts. The Italians engaged the two crippled merchants, and then took off in pursuit of the damaged *Partridge*. At 1420 hours, the Italian commander decided to break off the action. While the Italians did not destroy the convoy, only three ships reached Malta with 15,000 tons of cargo. The cost was high – the British lost a destroyer and two merchant ships, and a light cruiser, two destroyers, and a fleet minesweeper were all damaged by gunfire from the two RM cruisers. Only a single Italian destroyer suffered significant damage during the battle.

Bolzano was torpedoed by British submarine *Unbroken* off Panarea Island on August 13, 1942. The cruiser was run aground in an attempt to prevent her from sinking and is shown here afire and listing to port. *Bolzano* was eventually salvaged and moved to La Spezia for repairs, but never returned to service. (N. Siracusano collection)

Last Operations of the RM

The scant success of the two British June Malta convoys required that another major effort would have to be made. Both sides knew that the next convoy operation would decide Malta's fate. The British made a supreme effort with three carriers, two battleships, seven cruisers, and 24 destroyers to escort the large convoy of 14 merchant ships. The Axis gathered a large force of submarines, aircraft, and torpedo boats to attack the convoy as it approached from the west. The RM's ace card was a surface force of three heavy cruisers, three light cruisers, and 11 destroyers, with which it was planned to attack the convoy south of Pantelleria Island on the morning of June 13 after most of the British heavy ships had broken off in order not to risk a passage of the Strait of Sicily.

The battle of the "Pedestal" convoy was the largest battle of its type during the Mediterranean naval war. Losses to the convoy and its escorts were heavy – only five merchant ships reached Malta. The decisive moment of the entire battle might have been when the six RM cruisers attacked the decimated convoy. This was not to be. Only six hours before the moment of interception, the force was recalled by Mussolini. The decisive factor was a report that the convoy escort included a battleship which the RM cruisers could not have handled in a daylight action. Adding further insult, heavy cruiser *Bolzano* and light cruiser *Attendolo* were both torpedoed and heavily damaged by a British submarine while returning to base.

From this high point in August, Axis fortunes quickly declined. The Axis ground forces in Egypt were decisively defeated in late October at El Alamein, which was followed by landings in French North Africa by American and British forces. This massive operation changed the strategic balance in the Mediterranean. The focus of the naval war shifted to the convoy routes from Sicily to Tunis as the Axis struggled to supply its bridgehead in Tunisia. The RM's heavy units were unable to intervene because of a lack of fuel oil. Additionally, Allied airpower forced the Italian battle fleet to move to bases farther north to avoid attack. This was prompted by a December 4, 1942 attack on Naples by American heavy bombers which sank light cruiser *Attendolo* and damaged *Montecuccoli* and *Eugenio di Savoia*.

The destruction of Allied forces in Tunisia in May 1943 brought the Mediterranean naval war to its final phase. The RM's battle fleet of two battleships, three light cruisers, and 11 destroyers retained enough fuel for a final large-scale intervention, but this opportunity never came. The battle fleet did not intervene when the Allies invaded Sicily since lack of air cover and very unfavorable odds made any prospect for success doubtful. On September 8, 1943, the new Italian government signed an armistice. The following day, all units of the RM which could steam were ordered to depart for Allied ports. By this point, only two heavy cruisers remained, and these were both in a damaged condition. Nine light cruisers remained operational and eight reached Allied ports. For the remainder of the war, they acted under Allied control, conducting escort, transport, and training missions.

RM HEAVY CRUISERS

Trento Class

The first generation of RM heavy cruisers was the two-ship Trento class. The RM began to study a design for its first treaty cruiser after the Washington Naval Treaty was signed in February 1922 and in 1923 the design work was completed.

Trento-Class Construction

Ship	Built at	Laid down	Launched	Commissioned	Fate
Trento	Livorno	February 8, 1925	October 4, 1927	April 3, 1929	Sunk June 15, 1942 by British submarine *Umbra*
Trieste	Trieste	June 22, 1925	October 24, 1926	December 21, 1928	Sunk April 10, 1943 by USAAF

Like every other signatory to the treaty, the RM's design went up to the maximum allowed tonnage (and beyond) and carried the largest guns possible. As already mentioned, the RM favored high speed and firepower over protection, and the Trento class evidenced this. The long, flush-deck hull gave a graceful appearance. The main battery was configured in four twin turrets, two forward and two aft. This became the standard RM gun configuration for its heavy and light cruisers. The forward superstructure contained the bridge, and a tripod mast above it carried the main fire control directors. In early 1940, the two stacks were given funnel caps which further enhanced the ships' appearance.

Two large stacks indicated the presence of powerful machinery. The 12 boilers were placed in three separate spaces, and the turbines in two different spaces. The machinery produced 150,000 shaft horsepower, which was sufficient to drive the ship at a maximum speed of 31 knots. On trials, *Trento* achieved 35.6 knots, but this was not an indication of her operational speed

D The two ships of the Trento class were the RM's first heavy cruisers, commissioned in 1928 and 1929. Despite being the least well protected Italian heavy cruisers, they had fairly long wartime careers. The top and middle profiles show *Trento* as she appeared in April 1942; the ship was lost shortly thereafter in June. The starboard-side profile shows the cruiser's overall configuration, with a large bridge structure surmounted by a tripod mast with the main battery fire control equipment. The main battery is laid out in four twin 8-inch turrets, which became the standard RM heavy cruiser configuration. Note the absence of radar and the light scale of antiaircraft guns. The RM used a variety of camouflage schemes and *Trento* carries one of the more rare schemes designed by naval painter Rudolf Claudus. The intent was to alter the ship's appearance by projecting a shorter hull by use of a false bow and by applying saw-tooth patterns in a variety of colors. *Trento* was the only heavy cruiser to wear this pattern, which was applied in February–March 1942 and worn until the ship was lost. The overhead view shows the red and white aircraft recognition stripes applied to the forecastle of all RM combatants after the battle of Calabria. This was prompted by the performance of the Italian Air Force, since during the battle some 70 Italian aircraft bombed RM ships but achieved no hits.

The bottom profile shows *Trieste* in August 1942. This was her final configuration before her loss in April 1943 when the green areas on the bow and stern had been over painted in light gray. Her overall appearance is virtually identical to that of *Trento*, with the exception of additional 20mm guns placed on the forward superstructure and abaft the aft stack. *Trieste* also carried a striking camouflage scheme, which was the result of December 1941 regulations issued by the RM's Technical Department. These directed the use of dazzle camouflage. There were no standard designs; each ship had a unique pattern. The dazzle camouflage was based on the application of darker colors in one of three patterns. *Trieste* is wearing a straight-edged pattern. In August 1942, a light green replaced the white on the ship's bow and stern because experience had shown the white to be too conspicuous.

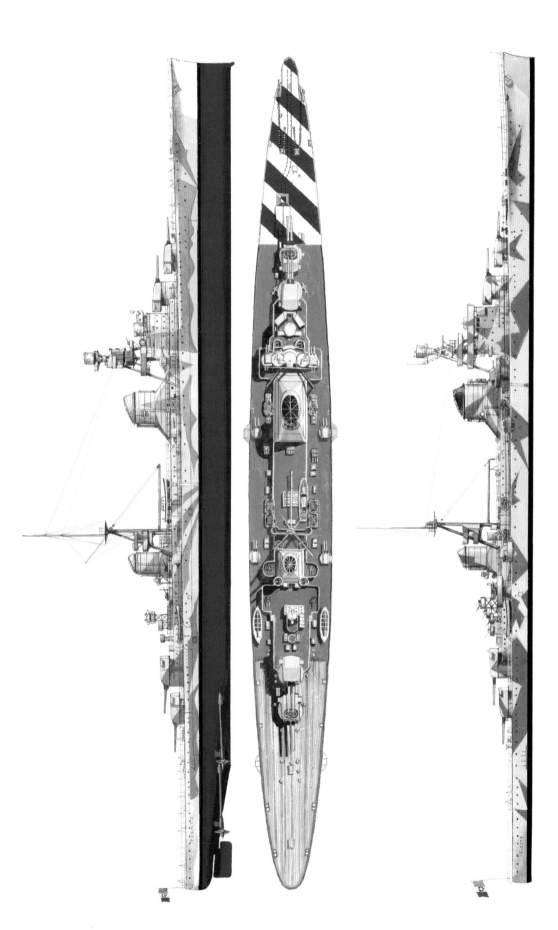

Trieste photographed probably at Messina in early March 1941. The ship retains her prewar configuration and overall light gray paint scheme. (E. Bagnasco collection)

since the trials were conducted under ideal conditions for the builder to collect a bonus for delivering a ship with a top speed over design specifications. Endurance was limited to 4,160nm at 16 knots, but this did not concern the RM since it planned to fight short-duration battles in the Mediterranean close to base.

Protection was insufficient for a large warship. The main belt, which ran between the forward and aft magazines, consisted of 70mm of armor; a transverse armored bulkhead of 40–60mm enclosed the vital spaces. The armored deck included a maximum of 50mm of armor from the forward hangar to the aft magazines. There was 20–30mm of armor aft to cover the steering spaces. The turret faces were given 100mm of armor, as was the conning tower. Barbette armor was 75mm thick.

An unusual feature was the placement of the ships' aviation facilities. After tests in the 1920s using a German prize cruiser from World War I, it was decided to put the catapult on the Trento class on the forecastle. There was room for two aircraft in a hangar forward and below the forward 8-inch gun turret. This arrangement proved impractical since it restricted the firing arc of the forward 8-inch gun turrets and because even in a moderate sea the aircraft placed on the catapult were exposed to damage.

Armament

The main battery consisted of eight 8-inch/50 guns mounted in twin turrets. Each gun was provided with 162 rounds. Secondary armament was originally 16 100mm/47 guns in eight twin turrets. They were placed four on the main deck and four on the superstructure. Original antiaircraft protection was provided by four single 40mm guns and four 12.7mm twin machine gun mounts. Additionally, a heavy torpedo battery was provided. This consisted of four fixed twin mountings on the main deck placed athwartships, with four tubes on each beam. The tubes were positioned between the two stacks and under the small aft control station.

In 1937, the two aft twin 100mm mounts were removed and replaced with four twin 37mm/54 mounts. By the start of the war, the 40mm guns had been removed and the 12.7mm guns replaced by four twin 13.2mm machine guns. During the war, both ships had their machine guns replaced by up to eight 20mm single guns.

This view of *Trento* from late 1940 shows the awkward arrangement of the ship's aviation facilities. An Ro.43, the RM's standard cruiser and battleship floatplane, is positioned on the bow catapult where it affected the forward 8-inch guns' arc of fire and was vulnerable to damage from heavy seas. (A. Fraccaroli collection)

Operational History

At the outbreak of war, both ships were assigned to the 3rd Division of the Second Squadron. Their usual base was at Messina on Sicily. Both were at Calabria in July 1940. *Trento* was at Taranto during the RN's air attack on the night of November 11–12, and was hit by a bomb, but damage was minimal since it failed to explode. *Trieste* was also present but was undamaged. Both fought at Cape Spartivento and Matapan. The remainder of 1941 and into 1942 saw both ships assigned to convoy escort duty. *Trento* was present at both battles of Sirte, and suffered damage from heavy seas on the second occasion.

On November 21, 1942, *Trieste* was torpedoed by British submarine *Utmost* while escorting a convoy to Libya but was able to return to Messina. In June 1942, *Trento* was part of the force which was tasked to attack a convoy moving from Alexandria to Malta. At 0500 hours on June 15 in the Central Ionian Sea, an RAF torpedo bomber hit *Trento* with a single torpedo which created a large fire in the forward boiler rooms and brought the ship to a halt. Attempts to tow the cruiser were unsuccessful, and at 0910 hours, RN submarine *Umbra* found the crippled cruiser and dispatched her with a torpedo which hit the forward magazines.

Trieste was repaired in time for the major air-sea battle surrounding Operation *Pedestal* in August 1942. She was sent to sea with a group of cruisers, but was recalled. On April 10, 1943, USAAF B-24s bombed her while moored in a bay near La Maddalena in Sardinia. Hit at 1345 hours, she capsized by 1613 hours. By 1950, the capsized hull was refloated and sent to La Spezia for scrapping. After the hull was righted and drydocked, the machinery was found to be in good condition, and the hull was sold to the Spanish Navy, which planned to convert it into a light carrier. By 1952, the ship had reached El Ferrol, but by 1956 the Spanish decided the project was too costly, so the hulk was sold for scrap in 1959.

Trento-Class Specifications

Displacement	Standard 10,500 tons; full 13,358 tons (*Trieste* 13,530)
Dimensions	Length 646 feet, 2 inches; beam 67 feet, 6 inches; draft 22 feet, 4 inches
Propulsion	12 boilers and four geared turbines generating 150,000shp on four shafts; maximum speed 31 knots
Range	4,160nm at 16 knots
Crew	781

Zara Class

The RM quickly realized that the Trento class was not a successful design because it was insufficiently protected. This shortcoming was especially important, as the RM's battleship force was viewed as ineffective since it was based on pre-World War I designs that had yet to be modernized. This

This well-known photograph shows an immaculate *Fiume* on May 5, 1938 in the Gulf of Naples during the naval review held for Adolf Hitler while on his state visit to Italy. The cruiser is proceeding at high speed with 8-inch turrets trained to port and is about ready to engage an unseen target. (Author's collection)

would place the RM's heavy cruisers in the battle line, something the Trento class was unable to do. The design specifications for the next class of heavy cruiser were to keep the eight 8-inch main battery, possess a top speed of 32 knots, but to increase protection to 200mm on the main belt. It was impossible to do all this on a 10,000-ton hull, so compromises had to be made. Since the RM was unwilling to compromise on the speed and firepower, this left protection.

Italian designers went to work on weight-saving measures that could be applied to the scale of protection. The flush-deck hull was abandoned, and a raised forecastle design adopted. This, and a hull shorter by some 90 feet, resulted in a 7 percent reduction in hull weight. The weight of the machinery was reduced by 9.3 percent by adopting a twin-shaft layout. Even when the main belt was reduced from 200mm to 150mm, the new cruisers were still well beyond the 10,000-ton limit. This varied from 11,300 tons for the lead ship to 11,900 for *Gorizia*.

The new design plans were completed in 1928 and the first ship laid down in early 1929. The last ship of the class was completed in late 1932.

Zara-Class Construction					
Ship	Built at	Laid down	Launched	Commissioned	Fate
Fiume	Trieste	February 22, 1929	April 27, 1930	November 23, 1931	Sunk March 28, 1941 by British battleships
Zara	La Spezia	July 4, 1929	April 27, 1930	October 20, 1931	Scuttled March 29, 1941
Gorizia	Livorno	March 17, 1930	December 28, 1930	December 23, 1931	Scrapped 1947
Pola	Livorno	March 17, 1931	December 5, 1931	December 21, 1932	Sunk March 29, 1941 by RN destroyers

Protection was increased and totaled 1,500 tons of armor. The main belt was 150mm at its thickest point. It stretched between the forward and aft magazine spaces and was closed off by a transverse bulkhead with between 90 and 120mm of armor. Horizontal protection was also increased to 70mm on the main armored deck and another 20mm on the upper armored deck.

E

The top profile depicts *Zara* as she appeared in June 1940 at the start of the war. The Zara class was a short-hull version of the Trento class, which employed a raised forecastle and other weight-saving measures to increase protection. At the start of the war, RM combatants wore a standard scheme of light gray on all vertical surfaces, dark gray on horizontal surfaces, and wood decking in its natural color.

The middle profile is *Gorizia* as she appeared in March 1942. Each of the Zara-class cruisers had minor distinguishing features; the main difference on *Gorizia* was the shape of her forward stack. The ship is wearing a sharp-edged dazzle camouflage pattern.

The bottom profile is *Bolzano* as she appeared in May 1942. Despite being a repeat of the Trento class, *Bolzano* displays several important differences. The flush deck was discarded to save weight, the size and shape of the bridge structure was modified, and the catapult was moved to a position between the two stacks. The splinter-pattern dazzle camouflage was applied in early 1942 and worn for the rest of the war. Like any dazzle scheme, it was designed to conceal the ship's true identity, course, and speed to observers. In August, the white on the extreme bow and stern was repainted in light gray.

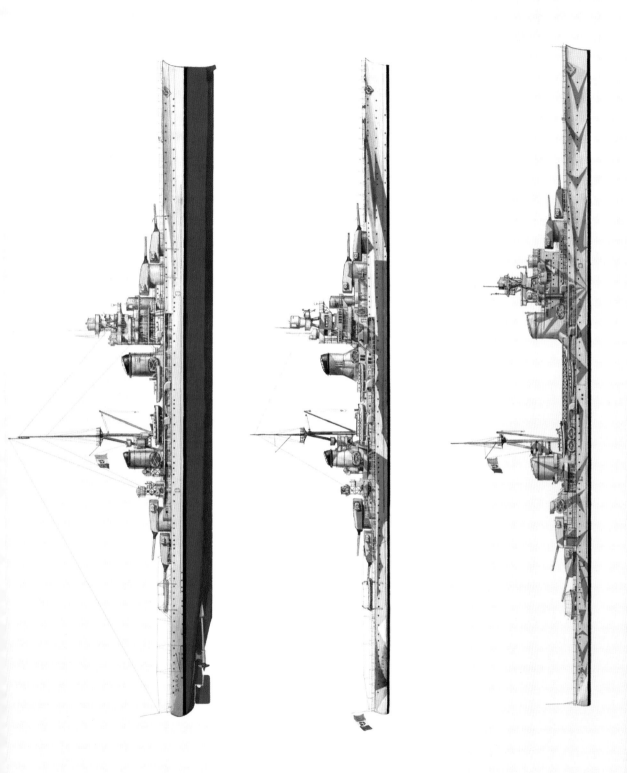

Other critical areas were well protected. There was 150mm of armor on the turret faces and the conning tower. Barbette armor was doubled to a maximum of 150mm.

Despite the greatly increased displacement, the cruisers achieved their design speed. As mentioned above, the scale of the machinery was reduced to eight boilers and two turbines to draft two shafts. The boilers were placed in five compartments, and both turbines were placed in separate spaces to increase resistance to damage. On trials, the ships produced speeds of up to 34 knots, but under actual service conditions their top speed was 30–31 knots.

This is the port side of *Pola's* bridge structure showing how the superstructure was faired into the forward stack. The extra space was used to accommodate an embarked staff in accordance with *Pola's* role as a flagship. Note the 4.7-inch/15 illumination howitzer on the platform abaft turret "B." This was one of the RM's few efforts to provide the training or equipment for night combat. (Istituto Luce, Rome)

Armament

The main battery consisted of eight 8-inch/53 guns mounted in twin turrets. The secondary remained at 16 100mm/47 guns in eight twin turrets. They were placed four on the main deck and four on the forecastle deck. In 1937, the aft pair of 100mm mounts was removed and replaced with four twin 37mm/54 guns. Antiaircraft protection varied from four to six single 40mm guns and four 12.7 twin machine-gun mounts. By the start of the war, the light antiaircraft fit totaled eight 37mm guns in twin mounts and eight 13.2mm machine guns in twin mounts. Because most of the class was lost in March 1941, modifications were minimal. *Gorizia* had the two 120mm/12 star shell guns fitted on the entire class early in the war replaced with two twin 37mm/54 mounts. It was planned to replace her 13.2mm machine guns with single 20mm/65 guns, but this was not done before the Italian surrender.

The heavy torpedo battery fitted to the Trento class was not repeated, but the unsuccessful arrangement of the aviation facilities was repeated.

Operational History

As the most capable RM heavy cruisers, these ships were considered integral parts of the battle fleet and were very active up until their loss. Cruisers of this class participated in every major operation. Three of the class were assigned to take part in the operation which led to the battle of Matapan. On the single night of March 29–30, 1941, all three were lost. *Fiume* and *Zara* were hit by 15-inch projectiles; *Fiume* sank at 2315 hours and *Zara* was scuttled by her crew by setting off explosions in the magazine and sank at 0240 hours

Fiume photographed sometime after 1937 as evidenced by the removal of the two aft twin 4.7-inch mounts and the fitting of twin 37mm/54 antiaircraft mounts. The cruiser is taking part in a review, making high speed with the crew manning the rails. (E. Bagnasco collection)

the following morning. *Pola* was lost in this same action after having been hit amidships on her starboard side by a single air-launched torpedo at 1950 hours on March 29. This hit brought her to a stop and started a chain of events which resulted in the destruction of two of her sister ships. The drifting *Pola* was dispatched by British destroyers at 0410 hours the following morning.

Gorizia was in the yards in March 1941 and missed Matapan. Following Matapan, she was based at Messina on Sicily and continued to be very active on convoy escort duty and battle fleet sorties in August and September 1941 and the First Battle of Sirte in December 1941. In March 1942, she was present at the Second Battle of Sirte and survived a series of air and submarine attacks during 1942 with only splinter damage. Her luck ran out on April 10, 1943 when USAAF bombers attacked the naval base at La Maddalena in Sardinia. Three bombs hit the cruiser, one of which penetrated 8-inch turret No. 3 and two of which hit forward. The cruiser was moved to La Spezia for repairs. At the time of the armistice, the ship was in drydock. The Germans seized the non-operational cruiser but made no attempt to complete repairs. On June 21–22, 1944, British and co-belligerent Italian frogmen penetrated La Spezia to sink *Gorizia* and *Bolzano* so they could not be used as blockships by the Germans. *Gorizia* survived this attack. In April 1945, the Allies found *Gorizia* still afloat in La Spezia but the decision was made not to repair her. The hulk was scrapped in 1947.

ABOVE LEFT
Gorizia photographed at Messina in early March 1942. The cruiser is wearing a transitional camouflage pattern between the early-war "Claudus" schemes to the standard dazzle patterns applied to most RM combatants from mid-1942. (G. Vaccaro collection)

ABOVE RIGHT
The stripped and half-sunk *Gorizia* photographed at La Spezia on June 15, 1946. The ship is still wearing her last splinter-pattern dazzle camouflage. The hulk was refloated and scrapped in 1947. (USAAF)

Zara-Class Specifications

Displacement	Standard 11,680 tons; full 14,300 tons (*Fiume* 11,326 tons standard, 13,944 tons full; *Gorizia* 11,712 tons standard, 14,330 tons full; *Pola* 11,545 tons standard, 14,133 tons full)
Dimensions	Length 557 feet, 2 inches; beam 62 feet, 10 inches; draft 20 feet, 4 inches
Propulsion	Eight boilers and two geared turbines generating 95,000shp on two shafts; maximum speed 32 knots
Range	Between 4,480 and 5,434nm at 16 knots
Crew	841

Bolzano

The design of the *Bolzano* was a step back for the RM since it was essentially a repeat of the under-protected Trento class. The nominal reason to build a single cruiser to this design was that it gave the RM a total of seven heavy cruisers; with the *Pola* operating as the fleet flagship until the modernized battleships entered service, this gave the Italians two three-ship heavy cruiser divisions. This also explained the reason that *Bolzano* was in many respects a repeat of the Trento class since it would allow the three ships to work together.

In reality, the driving reason behind the construction of *Bolzano* was to give Ansaldo a chunk of the heavy cruiser construction program since none of the first six were assigned to that firm. *Bolzano* was a graceful ship, but because of her insufficient protection she was unofficially described in the RM as "… a perfectly executed mistake."

Bolzano Construction

Ship	Built at	Laid down	Launched	Commissioned	Fate
Bolzano	Genoa	June 11, 1930	August 31, 1932	August 19, 1933	Sunk June 21, 1944 by British manned torpedoes

The design was based on the Trento class, but some modifications were incorporated. The general layout was similar in regards to the main battery, but the improved 8-inch guns from the Zara class were fitted. Among the weight-saving measures adopted was a forecastle instead of the flush-deck design of the Trento class. Despite this, *Bolzano* came in more than 1,000 tons over treaty limits.

Bolzano had a large forward superstructure, which, like *Pola*'s, extended back to and was faired into the forward stack. The unsuccessful arrangement of placing the aircraft catapult on the forecastle was abandoned, and a trainable catapult was placed between the two stacks. There was space to store three floatplanes, but only two were usually carried.

Speed returned as a design imperative; to attain the design speed of 33 knots, *Bolzano* was fitted with ten boilers and four turbines driving four shafts. The boilers were more powerful, so fewer were required. The ten boilers were placed in five compartments.

The penalty for increased speed was reduced protection. The main armor belt was only 70mm thick; horizontal protection was reduced to 50mm of armor. The conning tower was protected by 100mm of armor, and the face of the main turrets received 100mm with 80mm on the sides and roof. The turret barbettes received 60mm.

Armament

The main battery consisted of eight 8-inch/53 guns mounted in twin turrets; these were the improved version mounted on the Zara class. As on all previous RM heavy cruisers, the secondary battery consisted of 16 100mm/47 guns in eight twin turrets. As with previous RM heavy cruisers, in 1937, the aft pair of 100mm mounts was removed and replaced with four twin 37mm/54 guns. *Bolzano* went to war with eight 37mm/54 and eight 13.2mm machine guns, all in twin mounts. In 1942, 20mm single mounts replaced the 13.2mm machine guns.

Bolzano moored in the Gulf of La Spezia in March 1938. Though essentially a repeat Trento-class cruiser, she was built with the same bridge structure as *Pola* from the Zara class. (Photo A. Fraccaroli)

Bolzano photographed at La Spezia in June 1942 following repairs from a torpedo attack from British submarine *Triumph* on August 26, 1941. The ship is wearing a distinctive splinter-pattern dazzle camouflage scheme. (E. Bagnasco collection)

The heavy torpedo battery fitted to the Trento class was brought back, and the same arrangement was used. *Bolzano* also had provisions made to carry a large number of mines.

Operational History

Bolzano fought at the battle of Calabria and was hit by three 6-inch shells. These damaged her steering gear and hit her Number 2 8-inch turret, but the turret was able to continue firing. In November, she was present at Taranto but was undamaged by the British air attack. In 1941, *Bolzano* was present at Cape Matapan, and then covered convoys until the August operation to intercept a British convoy headed to Malta. On August 26, when returning from this unsuccessful interception operation, she was torpedoed by submarine *Triumph* north of the Strait of Messina. *Bolzano* was sent to Genoa for repairs which took until June 1942.

On August 12, 1942, *Bolzano* was part of a cruiser force sent to intercept the Pedestal convoy. The following day, she was hit by a torpedo from submarine *Unbroken*. Damage was heavy, and as a preventative measure, her forward magazines were flooded. *Bolzano* was beached on a nearby island and on September 15 was towed to Naples for inspection of the damage. In October, the ship was moved north to La Spezia for repairs. At this time, the RM considered converting her into a ship capable of launching aircraft over a flight deck which was to extend from her second stack to her bow, but this plan was never started because of higher-priority needs. When the Italians surrendered, the Germans found the hulk in La Spezia. On June 21–22, 1944, British and co-belligerent Italian frogmen mounted an attack on La Spezia during which *Bolzano* was sunk. The wreck was raised in 1949 and scrapped.

Bolzano Specifications

Displacement	Standard 11,065 tons; full 13,885 tons
Dimensions	Length 646 feet; beam 67 feet, 6 inches; draft 21 feet, 6 inches
Propulsion	Ten boilers and four geared turbines generating 150,000shp on four shafts; maximum speed 33 knots
Range	4,432 nm at 16 knots
Crew	788

RM LIGHT CRUISERS

Condottieri Class – *Da Barbiano* Group

The design of the RM's first class of what became known later as light cruisers was driven by their primary mission of performing scouting and by the development of large destroyers in the French Navy. The French ships entered service in 1922 and were equipped with 5.1- and 5.4-inch guns. They were larger, faster and better armed than RM destroyers of the period, and the design of the Condottieri class was in large measure to counteract them.

Condottieri Class – *Da Barbiano* Group Construction

Ship	Built at	Laid down	Launched	Commissioned	Fate
Alberico da Barbiano	Genoa	April 16, 1928	August 23, 1930	June 9, 1931	Sunk December 13, 1941 by British destroyers
Alberto di Giussano	Genoa	March 29, 1928	April 27, 1930	February 5, 1931	Sunk December 13, 1941 by British destroyers
Bartolomeo Colleoni	Genoa	June 21, 1928	December 21, 1930	February 10, 1932	Sunk July 19, 1940 by British surface ships
Giovanni dalle Bande Nere	Castellamare di Stabia	October 31, 1928	April 27, 1930	April 1932	Sunk April 1, 1942 by British submarine *Urge*

The ships were initially designated as "large scouts," which gives a clear indication of their design priorities. To gain the desired advantage in speed and firepower over the French large destroyers, protection was very limited. The ships had a straight bow and a forecastle extending to below the forward superstructure. Two widely spaced stacks, and the main battery fitted on two turrets each fore and aft, gave them a balanced appearance.

Speed was the foremost design requirement, and on trials the ships reached 40 knots. This was only possible under the most favorable conditions, and actual top speed in service was limited to 31–32 knots. Another implication of the imperative for high speed was a very high length to width ratio, which made the ships ride poorly in heavy seas. To save weight, the hull was lightly built. This resulted in severe vibration problems, which was problematic for the fire control systems. After entering service, some top weight was removed and the lower hull strengthened. This improved sea keeping, but the class still suffered from suspect seaworthiness. The ships were also very cramped and uncomfortable for the crew.

Protection was limited to 584 tons of armor. Plating 25mm thick was fitted over the machinery spaces and 20mm was placed over the magazines. There were also transverse armored bulkheads 20mm thick to enclose the vital areas. Horizontal protection was 20mm thick. The conning tower was provided with armor 40mm thick, and the face of the 6-inch turrets received 23mm of armor. This scale of protection was inadequate to stop even destroyer-sized shells, much less 6-inch shells from opposing light cruisers.

The ships were provided with aviation facilities, but they shared the same unsatisfactory arrangement as most of the RM's heavy cruisers. A catapult was fitted on the forecastle and a hanger had enough room for another floatplane.

Armament

The main battery consisted of eight 6-inch/53 guns arranged in four twin turrets. This gave the ships the capability to out-range the large French destroyers. A total of 1,800 shells were carried in the magazines. The secondary battery of 100mm/47 was fitted between the stacks in three twin turrets. By the start of the war, the light antiaircraft fit consisted of eight 20mm single guns and four twin 13.2mm machine-gun

Bartolomeo Colleoni photographed at Taranto in 1936. Not readily apparent in this view is the ship's very light scale of protection which led to all four of the Da Barbiano-class ships being lost. The seaplane on the bow catapult is a CANT 25 AR. (Foto De Siati, Taranto – M. Brescia collection)

mounts. A light torpedo battery of two twin launchers, one fitted on each beam, was also provided. In addition, the ships were fitted for mine-laying and could carry up to 111 mines.

Operational History

Da Barbiano was present at Calabria, but then was fitted for duties as a training ship. She was active in this role until December 1941, when it was decided to use her and *Di Giussano* to conduct a high-priority transport run to Libya with fuel and munitions. The British were aware of the mission, and dispatched four destroyers to intercept the cruisers. A clash off Cape Bon in Tunisia during the early hours of December 13 was calamitous for the Italians. *Da Barbiano* was hit by three torpedoes and sank quickly; one torpedo hit *Di Giussano*, which also sank quickly. *Colleoni*'s fate was similar. After being active early in the war conducting mine-laying and providing cover for convoys, she was sent to the Aegean in July 1940. En route, she was intercepted by an RN force of light cruiser *Sydney* (Australian) and five British destroyers. In the ensuing engagement on July 17, *Colleoni* was hit by three shells in the engine room, which brought her to a stop. The cruiser was finished off by torpedoes from the destroyers. *Bande Nere* was present at this engagement; after scoring a hit on *Sydney*, *Bande Nere* escaped. The cruiser was active throughout 1940 and into 1941 on convoy escort duties. In June, she and *Di Giussano* laid a minefield northeast of Tripoli; in December, these mines subsequently crippled the British surface force operating from Malta, sinking the British cruiser *Neptune* and damaging other ships. On March 22, 1942, *Bande Nere* participated in the interception of a British convoy bound for Malta. The cruiser was damaged by storms the following day en route to home port. Accordingly, she was sent to La Spezia for repairs, but on April 1, 1942, *Bande Nere* was hit by two torpedoes from *Urge* which broke the cruiser in two.

Alberto di Giussano photographed at Messina in late summer 1941 with an Ro.43 floatplane on the bow catapult. The ship did not receive a dazzle camouflage scheme before her loss in December, but the black tops of the stacks have been painted light gray to make the ship less conspicuous. (Gruppo ANMI Savona)

Condottieri Class – *Da Barbiano* Group Specifications

Displacement	Standard 5,200 tons; full 7,800–8,050 tons
Dimensions	Length 555 feet, 6 inches; beam 50 feet, 10 inches; draft 16 feet, 9 inches
Propulsion	Six boilers and two geared turbines generating 95,000shp on two shafts; maximum speed 31–32 knots
Range	3,800nm at 18 knots
Crew	521

Condottieri Class – *Luigi Cadorna* Group

It was immediately apparent that the preceding class of light cruisers was too fragile. While they were still under construction, the RM began design work on an improved version.

Bande Nere photographed at La Spezia in November 1941. The cruiser was one of the first RM combatants to receive a dazzle camouflage. *Bande Nere* was torpedoed on April 1, 1942 by British submarine *Urge* in the southern Tyrrhenian Sea. A single torpedo hit broke the ship in two, which sank quickly with a heavy loss of life. (E. Bagnasco collection)

The second group of Condottieri light cruisers did little to address the weaknesses of the first group. Stability was improved by lowering the bridge structure, but the two ships in the group remained largely unprotected. This is *Luigi Cadorna* in the late 1930s. (A. Fraccaroli collection)

Condottieri Class – *Luigi Cadorna* Group Construction

Ship	Built at	Laid down	Launched	Commissioned	Fate
Luigi Cadorna	Trieste	September 19, 1930	September 30, 1931	August 11, 1933	Stricken 1951; scrapped 1953
Armando Diaz	La Spezia	July 28, 1930	July 10, 1932	April 29, 1933	Sunk February 25, 1941 by RN submarine *Upright*

The dimensions of the new class were identical to those of the preceding one. The primary improvements were in stability and a stronger hull. The aircraft-handling facilities were moved from the forecastle to a position abaft the second funnel. This permitted the height of the forward superstructure to be reduced significantly. The aircraft-handling facilities now included a fixed aircraft catapult abaft the second stack; there was no hangar so the two floatplanes were stored on deck. The new catapult position eliminated the small aft superstructure, which resulted in a further saving of top weight.

Armament

The main battery remained as eight 6-inch/53 guns, but these were the improved 1929 Model and were fitted in larger turrets. The secondary battery of 100mm/47 guns was fitted between the stacks in three twin turrets, but in a different arrangement than the earlier class. By the start of the war, the antiaircraft battery consisted of eight 20mm single guns and four twin 13.2mm machine-gun mounts. These ships carried the same torpedo battery of two twin launchers and were also fitted for mine-laying and could carry between 84 and 138 mines, depending on the type carried.

Cadorna was modified in 1943 by having her catapult removed and replaced by two twin 20mm mounts. The following year, the torpedo mounts were also removed.

Operational History

The wartime employment of these ships reflected their marginal capabilities. Both were present at Calabria. *Cadorna* then went into reserve in February

Armando Diaz pictured during a goodwill visit to Australia in October 1934. The cruiser was sunk early in the war by a British submarine on February 25, 1941 while on a convoy escort mission. (M. Brescia collection)

This is a prewar photograph of *Armando Diaz* in La Spezia. Note the aircraft catapult has been moved to a position abaft the aft stack, a much superior arrangement than placing it on the bow. (A. Fraccaroli collection)

1941, but soon returned to service as problems mounted getting supplies through to Libya. In November–December 1941, the cruiser was used to transport fuel and munitions to North Africa. In January 1942, she was relegated to a training role. After a refit, she resumed active service in June 1943 and conducted transport and mine-laying missions. When Italy surrendered, she escaped to Malta and spent the rest of the war in Allied service. Following the end of the war, she was based in Taranto but never went to sea again. The aged cruiser was stricken in 1951 after serving as a stationary training ship. After participating in the battle of Calabria, *Diaz* was assigned to support convoys to Albania. In February 1942, she was assigned to cover a convoy to Tripoli, but was torpedoed and sunk by submarine *Upright* on February 25.

Condottieri Class – *Luigi Cadorna* Group Specifications

Displacement	Standard 5,316 tons; full 7,935 tons
Dimensions	Length 555 feet, 6 inches; beam 50 feet, 10 inches; draft 17 feet
Propulsion	Six boilers and two geared turbines generating 95,000shp on two shafts; maximum speed 31–32 knots
Range	3,000nm at 16 knots
Crew	521

Raimondo Montecuccoli Class – First Group

The RM continued to refine its light cruiser designs. In order to address the protection and strength issues, this new class was almost 50 feet longer and over 2,000 tons heavier. This allowed the design of the RM's first well-balanced light cruiser. It was also a very attractive ship with its two widely separated raked stacks and a small circular forward superstructure.

Raimondo Montecuccoli Class – First Group Construction

Ship	Built at	Laid down	Launched	Commissioned	Fate
Raimondo Montecuccoli	Genoa	October 1, 1931	August 2, 1934	June 30, 1935	Stricken 1964; scrapped 1972
Muzio Attendolo	Trieste	April 10, 1933	September 9, 1934	August 7, 1935	Sunk December 4, 1942 by USAAF

The most significant improvement was in the area of protection. The total weight of armor was increased to 1,376 tons, more than twice as much as the preceding class. The scale of armor protection was calculated to defeat 6-inch shellfire beyond 16,350 yards and 8-inch shellfire from beyond 25,000 yards. This equated to a main belt 60mm at its thickest point, with 40mm transverse bulkheads to enclose the vital spaces. Horizontal protection was increased to 30mm over the magazines and 25mm over the machinery

The badly neglected *Cadorna* as she appeared at Taranto in 1947. Following the end of the war, she never went to sea again and was used only for stationary training duties. (Photo A. Fraccaroli)

This 1937 photograph of *Montecuccoli* shows the ship's well-balanced and attractive configuration. This class introduced several new characteristics for RM light cruisers. Note the widely spaced stacks with the aviation facilities between them and the conical conning tower. (Foto Miniati, Leghorn – M. Brescia collection)

spaces. Barbettes were protected by between 30mm and 50mm of armor, and the conning tower received 100mm. The turret faces were protected by 70mm of armor.

A high speed was retained by using machinery capable of producing 106,000shp for a design speed of 37 knots. As was usually the case, service speed was considerably less, but was still a very respectable 33–34 knots. Most of the six boilers were placed in separate compartments, increasing resistance to damage.

The aircraft-handling facilities were positioned between the two stacks. A single trainable catapult was fitted and space for two floatplanes provided.

Armament

Though these two ships were much larger than the two previous light cruiser classes, there was no increase in firepower. The ships had their main battery fitted into four turrets, each with two 6-inch/53 guns. The secondary battery consisted of six 100mm/47 in twin mounts. The antiaircraft fit included

Montecuccoli (front) and *Duca d'Aosta* (rear) photographed at Brindisi in the winter of 1940–41. Note the difference in the conical bridge structure between the ships of these two classes. The four ships of the Montecuccoli and Duca d'Aosta classes were heavily employed in convoy escort and mine-laying operations during the war. (Photo A. Fraccaroli)

four twin 37mm/54 mounts forward and four 13.2mm twin machine-gun mounts. Two twin torpedo tube mounts were fitted amidships, one on each beam. The cruisers were also fitted with the capacity to carry a large number of mines – initially 112, and in 1941, this was increased to 146. The only known wartime modifications were the addition to *Montecuccoli* of eight 20mm/70 single mounts.

Operational History

The two ships of this class, together with the two ships of the largely identical Duca d'Aosta class, comprised the 7th Division and were staples in every major RM

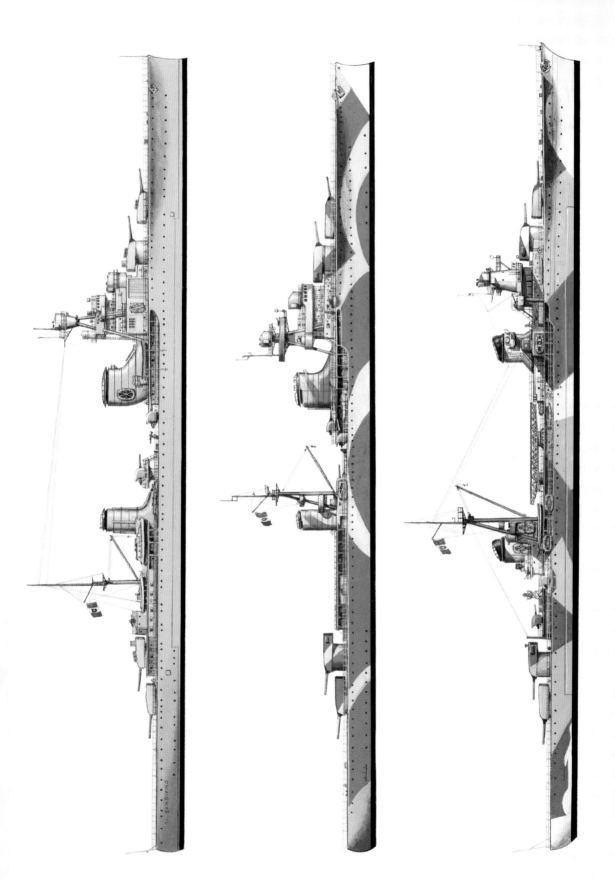

Muzio Attendolo pictured in late 1941/early 1942 with a "Claudus" camouflage scheme that she wore between July 1941 and July 1942. (E. Bagnasco collection)

fleet operation. Both were present at Calabria and were heavily used on convoy-protection and mine-laying missions.

Montecuccoli was damaged by USAAF bombers at Naples on December 4, 1942 by a single bomb that hit near the forward stack. The ship was towed to Genoa for repairs, which were not completed until July 1943. After the Italian capitulation, the ship reached Malta and was used as a fast transport until the end of the war. After the war, she was converted into a training ship until 1964 when she was stricken, and remained in reserve until 1972 before being scrapped.

Attendolo was assigned to the cruiser force to intercept the Pedestal convoy in August 1942, but she was torpedoed by submarine *Unbroken*, which blew off her bow. She eventually reached Naples where a new bow was fitted, but was sunk pierside there by a USAAF heavy bomber attack on December 4, 1942. The hulk was raised postwar, and consideration was given to rebuilding her as an antiaircraft cruiser, but nothing was done and the ship was scrapped in 1949–50.

Raimondo Montecuccoli Class Specifications	
Displacement	Standard 7,550 tons; full 8,995 tons
Dimensions	Length 597 feet, 9 inches; beam 54 feet, 6 inches; draft 18 feet, 4 inches
Propulsion	Six boilers and two geared turbines generating 106,000shp on two shafts; maximum speed 33–34 knots
Range	4,200nm at 18 knots
Crew	648

Duca d'Aosta Class (Raimondo Montecuccoli Class – Second Group)

The RM was pleased with the Montecuccoli class and decided to build two more near-repeat ships at the end of 1931.

Duca d'Aosta Class (Raimondo Montecuccoli Class – Second Group) Construction					
Ship	Built at	Laid down	Launched	Commissioned	Fate
Eugenio di Savoia	Genoa	July 6, 1933	March 16, 1935	January 16, 1936	To USSR March 1949
Emanuele Filiberto Duca d'Aosta	Livorno	October 29, 1932	April 22, 1934	July 13, 1935	To Greece July 1951

There were various minor improvements to the second group as compared to the first group of Montecuccoli-class ships. The new cruisers retained the same basic layout, but were some 16 feet longer and displaced almost 1,000

Attendolo was sunk on December 4, 1942 by USAAF heavy bombers in Naples. The ship was in port for repairs after suffering torpedo damage on August 13. *Attendolo* sank at her moorings and was not raised until August 1949 as shown here. After briefly being considered for rebuilding as an antiaircraft cruiser, the ship was scrapped. (F. Bargoni collection)

tons more. This provided room for the desired modifications, the primary one being the addition of extra armor. The total weight of armor went from the 1,376 tons on the Montecuccoli class to 1,700 tons on the new ships. The extra armor was distributed to the main belt, which was now 70mm at its thickest. Deck armor was increased to a maximum of 35mm, and turret face armor was increased to 90mm.

The only major difference in appearance was the configuration of the forward superstructure. The new class was fitted with a larger bridge to allow the ships to better act as flagships for an embarked staff of 42 men.

The machinery was upgraded to maintain the top speed of 33–34 knots even with the ship's increased displacement. The placement of the boilers was modified to increase resistance to damage; the six boilers were placed in groups of three, with each boiler in its own compartment.

Armament

In terms of fighting power, the two Duca d'Aosta-class cruisers were almost identical to the Montecuccoli class. The only difference was that while the earlier class was fitted with twin torpedo mounts, the two Duca d'Aosta-class ships carried triple mounts. Aircraft handling facilities were also identical, which allowed the ships to embark a maximum of three floatplanes. Wartime modifications were minimal – in 1943, both ships lost their torpedo tubes and aircraft-handling facilities and received ten 20mm/70 single mounts.

Operational History

The two ships of the Duca d'Aosta class were assigned to the 7th Division for much of the war and had a fine combat record. Both cruisers proved versatile in service, with a combination of high speed, mine-laying facilities, and good combat capabilities. Very importantly, they burned much less fuel oil than the larger heavy cruisers and battleships. Both ships were staples during the war, providing cover to convoys and conducting mine-laying operations in the Central Mediterranean.

Duca d'Aosta was present at the major fleet action at Calabria. Following a period of escort and mine-laying duties, the cruiser was present at the First Battle of Sirte. Her finest moment was at the battle of Pantelleria, when

she engaged a British cruiser and five destroyers. *Eugenio di Savoia* had a very similar early-war career, and was also present at Pantelleria. *Eugenio di Savoia* was earmarked to intercept the Pedestal convoy in August 1942, but the operation was canceled. The cruiser was at Naples on December 4, 1942 and was hit and damaged by USAAF bombers. After repairs, she rejoined *Duca d'Aosta* and both made abortive attempts on two occasions to bombard Allied forces on Sicily in August 1943. *Duca d'Aosta* was never damaged during the war and was considered to be the luckiest ship in the RM.

Both cruisers successfully reached Allied ports after the armistice was announced. *Eugenio di Savoia* was inactive, but *Duca d'Aosta* was given a refit, which included fitting an Allied radar, and was then assigned to blockade-runner interception duties in the Central Atlantic, operating out of Freetown from November 1944 to April 1945. After the war, the cruiser was laid up, and then given to the USSR on March 2, 1949 as reparations. The ship was renamed *Kerch* and served until 1959 before being scrapped. As part of the peace treaty with Greece, *Eugenio di Savoia* was ceded to Greece in 1951. Serving under the name *Helli*, she was taken out of service in 1964.

Duca d'Aosta Class Specifications	
Displacement	Standard 8,450 tons (*Eugenio di Savoia* 8,750); full 10,540 tons (*Eugenio di Savoia* 10,843)
Dimensions	Length 613 feet, 2 inches; beam 57 feet, 6 inches; draft 20 feet
Propulsion	Six boilers and two geared turbines generating 110,000shp on two shafts; maximum speed 33–34 knots
Range	3,900nm at 14 knots
Crew	694

Garibaldi Class

The final true RM light cruiser class represented a significant improvement over the two groups of the Montecuccoli class. The drive to lay down two more cruisers in 1933 was provided by the French Navy beginning construction on what would become a class of six light cruisers in 1931. The Garibaldi class was designed to be more than a match for the French cruisers,

while also being capable of engaging heavy cruisers. In order to do this, the RM sacrificed speed for more protection and firepower. The two ships of the Garibaldi class were laid down in 1933; both were launched on the same day in 1936 and entered service the following year. They were the best cruisers commissioned by the RM and both enjoyed long service lives.

Garibaldi Class Construction

Ship	Built at	Laid down	Launched	Commissioned	Fate
Luigi di Savoia Duca degli Abruzzi	La Spezia	December 28, 1933	April 21, 1936	January 12, 1937	Scrapped 1965
Giuseppe Garibaldi	Trieste	December 1, 1933	April 21, 1936	December 20, 1937	Scrapped 1978–79

Continuing the trend on the previous two classes, protection was a design requirement. The tonnage of armor was increased to 2,131, which was some 23 percent of standard displacement. This allowed side protection to be increased to an inner belt 100mm deep, which was fronted by a 30mm external belt designed to explode shells before they reached the main belt. The area of coverage by the main belt was decreased to the portion of the hull from the forward to aft magazines, which permitted the armored citadel to be given extra protection. The main deck armor was raised to 40mm, and an upper splinter deck with 15mm of armor was fitted. The armor protecting the conning tower was increased to 140mm, and the faces of the 6-inch turrets to 135mm. Overall armor protection was essentially equal to that of a Zara-class heavy cruiser.

The dimensions of the new ships were virtually identical to those of the previous class, but the beam was slightly increased. However, the appearance was altered significantly. The long, sweeping forecastle and quarterdeck were retained, as was the arrangement of the main battery. Instead of the two stacks being widely separated with the aircraft catapult placed between, the two stacks were placed together amidships. The forward superstructure was further increased in size, but the overall appearance remained sleek and balanced.

Despite the increase in displacement and a slight drop in power from the machinery to 100,000shp, top speed was still a respectable 31 knots. Both ships ran trials in a light condition and reached speeds of 33–34 knots, but in service the top speed was 31 knots. The eight boilers were placed in four separate spaces, but the arrangement was more compact, which saved weight and lessened the length of the hull that required armored protection.

Two turntable catapults were fitted and up to four floatplanes could be carried. The two catapults were fitted abeam the aft stack.

Armament

The Garibaldi class introduced the 6-inch/55 Ansaldo Model 1934, which placed each gun in an independent tray and increased the rate of fire to 5–6 rounds per minute. The number of guns in the main battery was increased to ten – triple mounts of the same type fitted on the Littorio-class battleships were fitted on a cruiser for the first time, with two twin mounts placed in a superimposed position. Secondary armament was four twin 4.7-inch/47 dual-purpose mounts. Antiaircraft protection was fairly light, with four twin 37mm/54 mounts and four twin 13.2 machine guns. A triple torpedo mount was provided on each beam. Wartime modifications were minimal – in 1942–43, ten 20mm/70 single mounts replaced the 13.2mm machine guns. *Abruzzi* received a German radar in August 1943.

Operational History

Both ships were present at Calabria in July 1940 but were spared the mainstay duties of most of the RM's other light cruisers – transport and mine-laying. Instead, the Garibaldi class was used in major fleet operations and to provide protection to convoys. Both were present at Matapan. On a convoy escort mission, *Garibaldi* was torpedoed by a British submarine on July 28, 1941. The torpedo hit in the area of the forward 6-inch gun turret and the resulting damage allowed 700 tons of water to enter the hull, but the ship survived and was repaired. *Abruzzi*'s turn to be tested by torpedo damage came on November 22, 1941, when she was hit by an air-launched torpedo in the stern which jammed her rudder. When the armistice came, both cruisers reached Malta to surrender. As the most capable Italian cruisers surviving the war, both were put to use by the Allies. Given British radars, both were sent to conduct anti-blockade-runner patrols out of Freetown, Sierra Leone, from November 1943 until April 1944 (*Garibaldi* serving only March to April in this capacity). Upon their return to Italy, both were used in transport and training duties until the end of the war.

Both ships had interesting postwar careers. When the Allies concluded a peace treaty with Italy in 1947, the two cruisers remained in Italian service and were the most capable units in the new Italian Navy. *Abruzzi* was refitted with new radar and antiaircraft guns, and served until 1961. *Garibaldi* was rebuilt between 1954 and 1961 and became the Italian Navy's first guided missile cruiser and flagship of the fleet. The missiles were provided by the United States, and the ship was also fitted with four tubes for Polaris ballistic missiles, but these were never provided. The ship was decommissioned in 1971 after serving 34 years.

The RM's surviving cruisers were placed at the disposal of the Allies after the Italian surrender in September 1943. This photograph shows *Abruzzi* at Taranto on April 29, 1944 following her deployment to the Atlantic to patrol for German blockade runners. Note the lattice mast abaft the bridge where a German radar is still in place. The catapult has also been removed and the ship's former dazzle scheme painted over. (E. Bagnasco collection)

G

The top profile is *Eugenio di Savoia* as she appeared in May 1942. She was the second ship of the Duca d'Aosta class and could be distinguished from the previous Montecuccoli class by a slightly larger bridge structure. The Duca d'Aosta class was almost a repeat of the previous class but incorporated additional protection. The splotch-pattern dazzle scheme on *Eugenio di Savoia* was modified in November 1942, when the white on the extreme bow and stern was painted over with dark gray.

The middle profile shows *Abruzzi* as she appeared in July 1942 in her dazzle scheme. *Abruzzi* was the second of the two Garibaldi-class light cruisers which were the last true light cruisers commissioned by the RM and were probably the RM's best overall cruiser design. The Garibaldi class can be distinguished from earlier light cruisers by their larger bridge and the two closely spaced stacks. Not evident in this profile are the two triple 6-inch gun turrets, making them the only RM cruisers to be fitted with a triple gun turret.

The bottom profile depicts *Attilio Regolo*, the first ship of the Capitani Romani class to be commissioned. The destroyer-like configuration of these ships is very evident, with their four 5.3-inch gun mounts, quadruple torpedo mounts, and a lack of aviation facilities. *Attilio Regolo* was given a splinter dazzle scheme when commissioned in May 1942 and was one of the few RM combatants to use green as one of the camouflage colors.

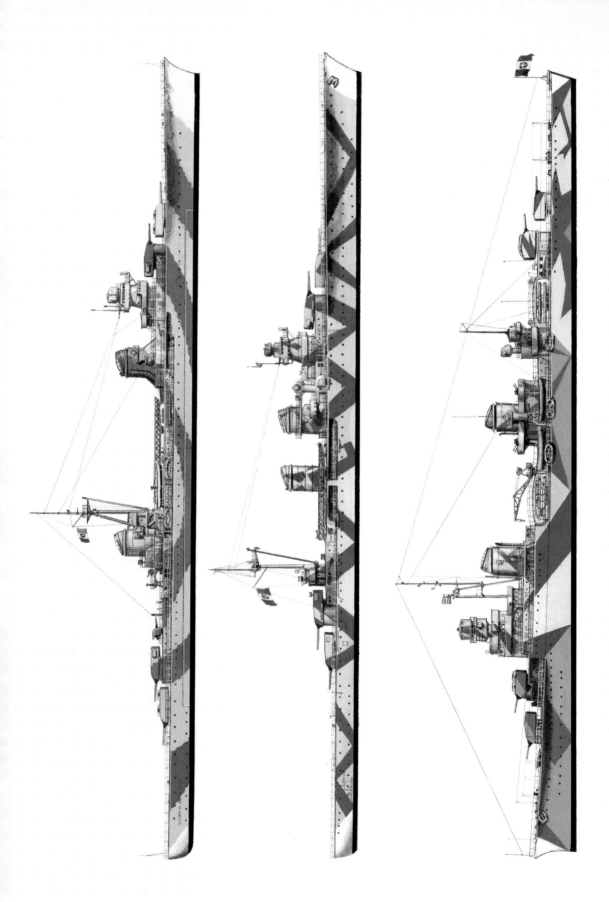

Giuseppe Garibaldi Class Specifications	
Displacement	Standard 9,195 tons (*Abruzzi* 9,592); full 11,528 tons (*Abruzzi* 11,542)
Dimensions	Length 613 feet, 6 inches; beam 62 feet; draft 20 feet
Propulsion	Eight boilers and two geared turbines generating 100,000shp on two shafts; maximum speed 31 knots
Range	5,360nm at 14 knots
Crew	850

Capitani Romani Class

The RM considered building another two modified Garibaldi-class light cruisers, but this was abandoned by 1940. This meant that the last class of RM light cruisers was actually something entirely different than another evolutionary Condottieri design. The new class, named Capitani Romani, was actually a large scout ship which had the armament, speed, and protection of a large destroyer, not a light cruiser. In fact, the RM called them "ocean scouts" (to avoid confusion with a class of large destroyers already in commission called "light scouts").

Capitani Romani Class Construction					
Ship	Built at	Laid down	Launched	Commissioned	Fate
Attilio Regolo	Livorno	September 28, 1939	August 28, 1940	May 15, 1942	To France August 1948
Giulio Germanico	Castellamare	April 3, 1939	July 26, 1941	1956 as *San Marco*	Stricken 1972
Pompeo Magno	Ancona	September 23, 1939	August 24, 1941	June 24, 1943	Stricken 1982
Scipione Africano	Livorno	September 28, 1939	January 12, 1941	April 23, 1943	To France August 1948

The design was based on the large destroyer *Tashkent*, which was built in Livorno and commissioned into Soviet service in May 1939. The lead contractor for the Capitani Romani class was the builder of *Tashkent*, so the firm used the 2,700-ton ship with a speed of 44.5 knots on trial as a basis for the new design. The requirement was for the new class, originally to number 12, to counter the fast and heavily armed French "super-destroyers" already in commission. The first ship was not laid down until April 1939, and only three ships ever saw service in the RM, with one being completed in 1942 and two in 1943. Thus, these ships played virtually no part in the war.

The ships emphasized high speed and were fitted with machinery to develop 110,000shp. This was sufficient to record 39–40 knots on trials and a very respectable 37–38 knots in operational service. They presented a handsome appearance, with a flush deck, two gun mounts fore and aft, and two widely spaced stacks. Protection was limited to splinter protection for the bridge area and 20mm of armor for the face of the gun mounts and 6mm on top.

Armament

The main battery of the new 5.3-inch/45 gun was fitted in four twin mounts. Antiaircraft weapons included four twin 37mm/54 mounts and eight 20mm/70 single mounts. A heavy torpedo battery of two quadruple mounts was fitted on the centerline. Facilities were provided to carry a maximum of 114–130 mines, depending on the type. The ships had no facilities for carrying aircraft.

This photograph shows *Scipione Africano* on October 1943 after taking Italian Marshal Badoglio to Malta. The cruiser was one of the few RM combatants to receive radar, which can be seen atop the tripod mast. (NARA)

Pompeo Magno photographed in July 1943. With almost no protection, this class was a step back for Italian light cruiser design. Note the empty position on top of the tripod mast where a "Gufo" radar was planned to be added. (A. Molinari collection)

Operational History

Since these ships entered service late in the war, their operational service was limited. The lead ship in the class, *Attilio Regolo*, was commissioned in May 1942. On November 8, she was torpedoed by a British submarine and lost her bow. She was towed to La Spezia, where the bow was replaced with that from one of her uncompleted sister ships. Upon completion of the armistice, *Attilio Regolo* made for Malta, but was ordered to assist in the rescue of crewmen from the sunken battleship *Roma*. She then headed to the Balearic Islands where she was interned until January 1945. Following the war, she was allocated to the French Navy on August 1, 1948, serving until 1962. The ship was scrapped in 1970.

The second ship of the class to be commissioned, *Scipione Africano*, was ordered to transit the Strait of Messina to reach Taranto on July 16, 1943. The cruiser made the transit safely at full speed, encountering four British torpedo boats, sinking one and damaging two. Operating from Taranto, she laid two minefields in August. After the Italian surrender, she conducted transport and training missions under Allied control. In August 1948, she was handed over to the French Navy and served under her new flag until 1961 before being scrapped.

The final ship to commission into RM service, *Pompeo Magno* was only in service for three months before the surrender. She was also allocated to France as a war reparation and was stripped of equipment and machinery by the French Navy. However, she remained in Italian control and between 1953 and 1955 was rebuilt and recommissioned as *San Giorgio*. She returned to the yards for further modernization from 1963 to 1965 and returned to service as a training ship, serving until 1982. *Giulio Germanico* did not commission before the Italian surrender. After the war, she was refloated and rebuilt between 1953 and 1956 as a training ship. Upon entering service, she was renamed *San Marco* and served in this capacity until 1972.

Capitani Romani Class Specifications

Displacement	Standard 3,084 tons; full 5,420 tons
Dimensions	Length 468 feet, 9 inches; beam 47 feet, 3 inches; draft 16 feet
Propulsion	Four boilers and two geared turbines generating 110,000shp on two shafts; maximum speed 37–38 knots
Range	4,300nm at 17 knots
Crew	420

Ex-German Cruisers from WWI

Three German light cruisers were allocated to the RM as war reparations and were handed over in 1920. All were given extensive overhauls and provided useful service. *Ancona* was decommissioned in 1937, but *Taranto* and *Bari* were still active during World War II. *Taranto* was the former German *Strassburg*, which was completed in 1912. Before entering Italian service, she was re-equipped with seven 5.9-inch guns. Designated as a light cruiser in 1929, the ship was used primarily in East African colonial duties. By the start of the war, her speed had been reduced to 20–21 knots, which made her suitable only for secondary duties like mine-laying and supporting ground operations along the Yugoslavian coast. The aging cruiser was assigned to the "Special Naval Force" in late 1940, which was being assembled for amphibious operations in Greece and later Malta. *Taranto* was decommissioned in December 1942. On September 9, 1943, the ship was scuttled by its crew in La Spezia.

Bari was the former German *Pillau*, which was completed in 1914. She was also re-armed with 5.9-inch guns (in this case eight) and assigned to colonial duties from 1934 to 1937. *Bari* had a fairly eventful wartime career since she had been converted to use fuel oil in 1934 and still retained a top speed of 24 knots. At the start of war, the cruiser was assigned as flagship of the Special Naval Force in 1940 and was slated to lead the abortive landings on the Greek island of Corfu in November 1940. She did conduct convoy escort duties to Greece, operations along the Yugoslavian coast in early 1942, and took part in the Italian occupation of Corsica in November 1942. Had the amphibious landing on Malta occurred as planned in 1942, she would have been present there. In January 1943, the RM placed the cruiser in reserve at Livorno with the intent of converting her into an antiaircraft cruiser. The work had not begun when *Bari* was sunk in shallow water by a USAAF bomber raid on June 28, 1943. The wreck was not repaired and was scrapped in 1948.

ANALYSIS AND CONCLUSION

From a design perspective, the RM's cruisers were an uneven lot. As was the case with all the naval powers that struggled to build balanced ships in the face of treaty restrictions, the first Italian cruisers were decidedly unbalanced. However good RM cruiser designs were, the Italians struggled with other factors which determined how effective a cruiser was in combat. These included fire control and gunnery technologies, antiaircraft capabilities, and radar. In all these areas, the RM began the war in a position of inferiority and never caught up.

RM heavy cruiser designs were fully the equal of French and British heavy cruisers. The Zara class was undoubtedly the best RM heavy cruiser. The class suffered heavily on a single night at the hands of the British Royal Navy, but no heavy cruiser could have withstood 15-inch shells at point-blank range. The Zara class was considered as mini-capital ships by the RM and at one point was classified as armored cruisers. The first generation Trento class was disappointing in service, and the similar Bolzano class was quickly seen as a mistake. For an additional two knots of speed, Bolzano sacrificed too much in the area of protection. It must be noted that all three classes came in over treaty limits. This did not upset the Italians, who were aware of this violation from the onset.

In service, RM heavy cruisers proved they were not able to withstand damage. No ship survived more than one torpedo hit.

Fate of RM Heavy Cruisers

Prewar total	Sunk by surface action	Sunk by submarine or manned torpedo	Sunk by air attack	Surviving
7	3	2	1	1

The first two classes of Condottieri light cruisers were poor designs and were derided by even the Italians before the war began. In their effort to match the speed of the large French destroyers, Italian designers gave up any pretense of producing a balanced cruiser. The cruisers possessed insufficient protection to stop even destroyer-sized gun shells. In addition, they exhibited poor sea-keeping characteristics, which meant they were not stable gun platforms. They possessed some utility in hit-and-run and transport missions, but were not useful in fleet actions. After being assigned to the main fleet early in the war, they were removed by 1941 and assigned to special missions. The performance of these first six Condottieri ships confirmed their susceptibility to damage. Only one of them survived the war.

The RM was aware that its light cruisers were excessively fragile. The next six ships of the Montecuccoli, Duca d'Aosta, and Garibaldi classes were much improved, and possessed levels of protection comparable or better than many foreign contemporaries. They remained active with the main fleet until the end of the war. Of the six cruisers, five survived the war.

Fate of RM Light Cruisers (does not include *Bari* or *Taranto*)

Ships	Sunk by surface action	Sunk by submarine	Sunk by air attack	Surviving
Prewar (12)	3	2	1	6
War-built (3)	0	0	0	3

Nevertheless, whatever their shortcomings, RM cruisers were an important part of a fleet which was largely successful in achieving its wartime objectives. The RM kept Axis forces in North Africa supplied. Of the cargos and personnel loaded in Italian ports, 90 percent and 98 percent arrived at their destinations, respectively. Additionally, the RM succeeded in blocking the Sicily Strait to British merchant traffic, which forced the British to route convoys around the Cape of Good Hope instead of through the Mediterranean. This had worldwide implications for the availability of Allied shipping. The RM paid a heavy price for this, for example losing 14 of its total of 24 cruisers, but by the end of the war the RM still existed as a coherent fighting force. The same cannot be said of the other Axis navies.

BIBLIOGRAPHY[1]

Bagnasco, Erminio and Brescia, Maurizio, *La Mimetizzazione Della Navi Italiane 1940–1945 (Italian Navy Camouflage 1940–1945)*, Tuttostoria, Parma, Italy (2006)

Bragadin, Marc' Antonio, *The Italian Navy in World War II*, Naval Institute Press, Annapolis, MD (1957)

Brescia, Maurizio, *Mussolini's Navy*, Naval Institute Press, Annapolis, MD (2012)

Gay, Franco and Valerio, *The Cruiser Bartolomeo Colleoni*, Conway, London (1987)

O'Hara, Vincent P., *Struggle for the Middle Sea*, Naval Institute Press, Annapolis, MD (2009)

Sadkovich, James P., *The Italian Navy in World War II*, Greenwood Press, Westport, Connecticut (1994)

1   Note: For reasons of space, we can list here only a select bibliography. A fuller bibliography can be found on the Osprey website by following: www.ospreypublishing.com/nvg_258_bibliography

INDEX